Unity

The Place of Commanded Blessing

by
Sharon D.C. Rich

Copyright © 2008 by Sharon D.C. Rich

Unity
The Place of Commanded Blessing
by Sharon D.C. Rich

www.RICHMINISTRIES.com

Printed in the United States of America

ISBN 978-1-60477-275-3

All rights reserved solely by the author. The author guarantees all contents are original and do not infringe upon the legal rights of any other person or work. No part of this book may be reproduced in any form without the permission of the author. The views expressed in this book are not necessarily those of the publisher.

Unless otherwise indicated, Bible quotations are taken from the King James Version of the Bible.

First print 2002 as Unity
Second print 2004 as Unity

Editor – Caroline Coley

www.xulonpress.com

Unity

~ *Dedication* ~

This book is dedicated to my father, *Matthew Collins Jr.*, for your faithfulness and diligence through the years in providing for my mother, my fifteen siblings (*Charlotte, Rochelle, Asa, Matthias, Allen, Sally, Craig, Clarence, Jonathan, Elizabeth, Curtis, Sherman, Philheus, Alma,* and *Micah*) and me. Thank you for being a role model father, serving both in ministry and in the United States Navy (God and country). You have always demonstrated great strength, shouldering such an incredible amount of responsibility with the greatest of ease. Because you were always there, and the role you have played in my life, I've never had to look for a hero. You are my hero. Thank you also for your blessing upon my life and this book.

In Memory
of
"Momma"
Millie Collins
July 30, 1943 – December 4, 2004

Who can find a virtuous woman? For her price is far above rubies.
Her children arise up, and call her blessed; her husband also, and he praiseth her.
Many daughters have done virtuously, but thou excellest them all.
Proverbs 31:10, 28, 29

Breathing is not the same without you.

Special Thanks
to
LaMont, LaMonique, Ryan, Mark, Tricia, Jack and Joshua

~ *Table of Contents* ~

Introduction	ix
Chapter I Tools of Division	13
Gossip among Christians	13
Wheat and Tares	18
Grow on to Maturity	20
Chapter II The Early Church	23
Pavements of Suffering	23
Felicitas	26
Martyrs for Christ	27
Today's Persecuted Church	29
God's Check and Balance System	33
Grounds of Division	36
The Perfecting of the Saints	37
A Word from the Lord	39
Win the Lost	41
Chapter III David	43
A Father's Plea	43
David's Sons	48
Son's of God	56

    Groups of Christianity..57
    I Am The Way 64
    Subduing Division 67
    The Call to Unite..70

Chapter IV   Moses 73
    Desert Travel..75
    Promise Land Hindrances 78
    Preparing the Priest and Tabernacle..................................85
    Clothing the Priest..94
    The Most Holy Place 95
    The Wise Hearted Menders...97
    The Church at Large 100

Chapter V   Joshua...101
    The Seventh Day..101
    Loyalty..103
    The Place of Commanded Blessing 104
    Empowered Through Submission 107
    The Captain of the Host 109
    Our Seventh Day..113

~ *Introduction* ~

The original thought of this book is from Psalm 133:1-3.

> 1 Behold, how good and how pleasant it is for brethren to dwell together in unity!
> 2 It is like the precious ointment upon the head, that ran down upon the beard, even Aaron's beard: that went down to the skirts of his garments;
> 3 As the dew of Hermon, and as the dew that descended upon the mountains of Zion: for there the LORD commanded the blessing, even life for evermore.

It is through Psalm 133:1 that a revelation of God is found concerning David. The second verse contains a revelation of God regarding Moses and finally the third verse gives light to the grace of unity that Joshua experienced.

Webster defines **Unity** as *a state of being one; concord agreement; harmony; artistic harmony and symmetry.*

This is the hour God is combining key elements from every portion of His body. This combination is similar to the commandment God gave Moses to take the principle spices of myrrh, cinnamon, calamus, cassia, and olive oil compounded after the art of the apothecary. The holy ointment was used to anoint the tabernacle and all that was within, and also Aaron and his sons as recorded in Exodus 30: 23-31.

If we look at the different expressions of the body of Christ it is quite easy to see God has anointed His vessels within their specific areas of expertise in ministry. Whatever portion of the body of Christ you serve; whether your expertise is administration, deliverance, helps, healing, faith, finances, family, prison ministry, education, worship, the arts, leadership, discipleship, consecration, or biblical revelation, God has anointed you to be a principle spice used to make up His anointing oil.

The process of making the oil involved compounding rare and rich spices, infusing them in oil, straining them (removing their individuality, but retaining their essence) out of the oil which produced a sweet smelling ointment.

Visit almost any church today and poll its members about the denomination from which they originated, and you will find a mixture of denominations represented. The denominations represent various spices mixed and compounded together and placed in oil (symbolic of anointing), strained, and now have become a unified ointment with a combined sweet fragrance that God uses as a tool to approach Himself.

After God commanded Moses to make the original ointment, to anoint the vessels and the priest, He instructed him to make a perfume that would serve as incense (Exodus 30:34-36). The use of this incense is seen in Leviticus 16:12 where God commands Aaron to take a censer full of burning coals from the altar before Him. Upon entering the Most Holy Place the priest, having hands full of sweet incense and bearing the censer, from which the combined incense placed on the coals produced a covering (cloud), was allowed access into the Most Holy Place. This entrance into the room housing the mercy seat, where God would meet with man, allowed Aaron to make atonement for the sins of the people.

In this hour God has combined spices from various parts of the body of Christ. The body of Christ has also completed a time when God allowed ministries to be placed upon coals of hot fiery trials. We, the body of Christ, are standing at the threshold of a dimension of God only experienced when the cloud fills the room. The cloud of glory that the combined spices and trials have produced is so splendid that no flesh will glory in His presence. It is this dimension of glory that will give us access (grace) to realms of God we have not experienced, on a large scale, before in the earth.

I believe unity is the key element God is using in our day to unlock a supernatural and miraculous move, which will escort us into a manifestation of the power of God that can't be traced back to the hand of man. Therefore, there is a great cry of the Spirit for the body of Christ to unite forces.

Many efforts are made to unite the body of Christ through conferences and behind the scene efforts of leaders, yet there are many opposing forces. If we are to see the genuine manifestation of the Spirit of God in our day sweep across the globe we must bridge the gaps created by opposing forces and unify our gifts, talents, callings and expertise in ministry so that we may dwell in **The Place of Commanded Blessing — Unity**.

If we are to take full advantage of this kingdom moment it would serve us to know:

The tool of the enemy that is posing as a potential threat to our imminent victory in examples seen through TOOLS OF DIVISION, the pavements of suffering in the lives of THE EARLY CHURCH, the revelation of Unity through the lives of three key individuals DAVID, MOSES and JOSHUA.

I sincerely desire as you read this book that the light of God will illuminate facets of unity in your spirit that will cause you to forever be a tool of UNITY for His glory.

Chapter I

Tools of Division

From the Early Church to our present day, one common thread has held the church together. Our belief that God, Jehovah, is our God and that we are redeemed and justified through Him by Christ Jesus His Son. Jesus came to earth, born of a virgin, died in the likeness of sinful flesh and rose from the dead. The same Jesus, being the perfect sacrifice has reconciled us back to the Father. This foundational belief has served as the one common thread throughout the ages that ties the church of the Lord Jesus Christ together.

If we are to walk in unity we, the body of Christ, must be aware of the devices of the enemy that serve as tools of division. We must be ever mindful that *every kingdom divided against itself is brought to desolation.*

Regardless of our differences, the fact we believe Jesus came as the propitiation for our sins, and our acceptance as the atonement, His sacrifice of shed blood and death for the remission of our sins, engrafts us into the beloved body of Christ.

Today there are major attacks against unity in the body of Christ. For example, love, which produces unity, has received a major attack. The strategic attack against love has caused Christians to be vulnerable to a weapon utilized by the kingdom of darkness - division. Tools of the kingdom of darkness ranging from outside forces raising accusations that cause one to question the integrity of a brother or sister - to doctrinal issues - to blatant attacks unwisely spoken in a moment of offense, serve as tools of division among us.

Regardless of our past shortcomings in unity and love, the Lord is yet commanding that we, the body of Christ, love one another. Jesus spoke so passionately when He said:

"By this shall all men know that ye are my disciples, if you have love one to another." (John 13:35)

The same depth of love Jesus commanded His disciples to have is a command to His body today. Love one to another is the essential element required for the body to function properly as one.

Is it possible that the world (unbelievers) possess a greater understanding than the church that we are one? Have you ever noticed when a part of the body of Christ has an unfavorable report aired by the news media, the entire body of Christ is placed under a microscopic view in an unfavorable light? When people that are either atheist or non-practicing Christians approach you about the exposed fall of a "Religious" public figure, they will in their summation say sarcastically, *"They're all like that. That's why I don't go to church."*

Just think about it, whenever the body of Christ has suffered humiliation due to an exposed sin of one of our brothers or sisters, the summation of the world's view is that the "Church" (a.k.a. religious people, or Christians) has fallen, not a denomination, not a particular ministry, not a race, nor a gender but the Church.

Most of us could think of a scandal that has occurred in the body of Christ without any hesitation. Therefore, there isn't any reason to mention any one incident. The scandalous headlines and special reports that have served as food to those with gluttonous appetites for negative reports have been far too many. Spouses, children, friends, staff members, church members, and supporters of such ministries have suffered major emotional scars that can only be healed by His nail-scarred hand.

~ *Gossip among Christians* ~

As is often the case, when people repeat unfavorable information among the body of Christ, they will clothe their gossip with the mask, "I'm sharing this only because I want you to pray about the situation, it is heavy on my heart." In public settings, on a larger scale, during a testimony, sermon, or teaching one may say, "I am using this solely as an illustration of how sin subtly overtakes individuals." One question that we may ask ourselves while examining our motives is would I want someone to repeatedly relay my greatest sin because I need prayer and I am heavy on their heart, or display my shame to make an illustration? I find that people who *really* travail in prayer for others usually do not require a lot of information about the situation to pray. A basic request for prayer such as "There is a brother/sister who is going through a major attack from the enemy and I am requesting your prayers for him/her and those concerned" will usually suffice for those who will pray. Likewise, those who are in need of an example of how sin subtly overtakes individuals can find so many life changing examples in the word of God that it is not necessary to exploit the downfall of a brother/sister who has been overtaken in a fault or sin.

I want to challenge you when approached by individuals relaying unfavorable information, to step to the spiritual plate and break the cycle of gossip by saying "You know, I don't have to have all of the details. Let's just pray right here and now." Pray a fervent prayer. If the person actually has been overtaken in a fault or sin, agree that their sins are remitted (John 20:23) and bind any means that would give voice to the incident, serving as a carrier of the word of reproach. Thereafter, confess and decree by faith that your *brother/sister* is now receiving a heart of true repentance. Agree that God is bringing to their aid counselors, mentors and intercessors to cover and assist them, so they are never again overtaken in the fault or sin. Furthermore, agree they are being restored to their rightful place in the body of Christ, growing on to maturity and doing great exploits for His glory.

In this life we are given many opportunities to perfect the skill of forgiving the faults and sins of others. We should always sow love and mercy, considering our own frailties lest we fall into the same snare. The scripture states that love covers (hides) a multitude of faults and sins.

The Christian form of covering a fault or sin is targeting the person at fault in prayer and not gossiping about the incident. While you are covering the fault or sin in prayer the pastoral team or persons in leadership, having the authority to speak into the life of the individual, will search out the matter and apply the required correction. This form of correction varies greatly according to the incident, the heart of the offender towards repentance, and their role in the church.

Considering scandals, we could chalk-up the EXTRA venomous broadcasting of such incidents as being the devil, his imps, and his kids doing what they love to do, attempting to divide and bring shame upon the body of Christ. However, we must not blame the devil or his helpers for the role that Christians have played in giving information to the media, slander magazines, journalists, newspapers, gossip columnists, web-sites, or other mediums used to spread unfavorable news.

There were incidents of sin associated with the church that the media took the opportunity to broadcast, rebroadcast and broadcast again mercilessly. The major reporters stated that in those cases they did not have to research extensively, because "CHURCH PEOPLE" called, faxed and mailed in information. That is a form of Body Exposure, where the body uncovers another part of the body's frailty, sin, fault, or shame.

The reasoning behind such actions are usually wrapped in *religious* statements such as "God needed someone to speak up and bring to light heresy in the church, sin in the church, what's been done in the dark, and wolves in sheep clothing leading others astray." Some people have even created entire "ministries" where the sole purpose is to expose what they consider as wrong doings in the body of Christ.

It is always very painful to observe the body devouring the body. Whether reading about an unfavorable incident in a Christian magazine or becoming exposed to the incident through some other source, there is a type of pain and shame that accompanies the news. These feelings are greatly coupled when the news is reported as information submitted by another Christian, especially if the person acquired the information during a covenant relationship with the individual. It is the same type of pain and shame that I feel when something negative happens associated with a close loved one or family member. In those moments I live through the whole experience of the lump in the throat and the hesitancy to talk with those who may use the occasion to covertly gloat over the misfortune or the shame of my loved one. My feelings may be viewed as overly sensitive; however, I feel I have been given this sensitivity for His purpose.

I view the act of the body spreading unfavorable incidents about another portion of the body of Christ as a physical body turning and devouring itself. It is interesting that if we see a dog foaming at the mouth intently pursuing his tail, with the intent to devour it, we will categorize that dog as a mad dog, and avoid any contact. However, some Christians entertain conversations of slander with people who are known for spreading malicious gossip about believers without a thought to the damage that such behavior inflicts upon the body of Christ.

When Christians relay unfavorable reports, they are in fact damaging themselves, the hearer, and the person/ministry that the gossip refers to. It is an act of the body devouring the body. The enemy has often used this type of slander as a tool of persecution. The intent is to stop the righteous influence of the Church.

It's important for us to be aware that nothing spoken about the body of Christ is neutral. Every report passed along is either causing our sphere of influence to increase or decrease.

~ *Wheat and Tares* ~

I do not by any means want to give the impression that I am a flower child skipping through the tulips with the perception that every one naming the name of God is holy, possessing a pure heart, and raising up ministries that are produced from the seed of God. I, like you, am painfully aware that there are "ministries" that are not of the seed of God in the world.

Jesus spoke concerning tares, the ungodly, of the world in Matthew 13:24-30:

> *"Another parable put he forth unto them, saying, The kingdom of heaven is likened unto a man which sowed good seed in his field: But while men slept, his enemy came and sowed tares among the wheat, and went his way. But when the blade was sprung up, and brought forth fruit, then appeared the tares also. So the servants of the household came and said unto him, Sir, didst not thou sow good seed in thy field? From whence then hath it tares? He said unto them,*

An enemy hath done this. The servants said unto him, Wilt thou then that we go and gather them up? But he said, Nay; lest while ye gather up the tares, ye root up also the wheat with them. Let both grow together until the harvest: and in the time of harvest I will say to the reapers, Gather ye together first the tares and bind them in bundles to burn them: but gather the wheat into my barn."

Later after Jesus sent the crowd away, His disciples, those who were close to Him in a covenant relationship, asked Him to unveil the revelation concerning the tares of the field. Jesus replied in Matthew 13:37-41.

"...He that soweth the good seed is the Son of man; The field is the world; the good seed are the children of the kingdom; but the tares are the children of the wicked one; The enemy that sowed them is the devil; the harvest is the end of the world; and the reapers are the angels. As therefore the tares are gathered and burned in the fire; so shall it be in the end of this world. The Son of man shall send forth his angels, and they shall gather out of HIS kingdom all things that offend and them which do iniquity."

Jesus revealed to his disciplined ones the knowledge of tares that are sown into His field (world) while men tended to their natural needs. During their sleep, which speaks of a state of being unconscious of spiritual activity or being absorbed by the cares of this life, the devil came and sowed tares in the world. The workers of the field, whose job was to tend the field, asked the owner should they uproot (remove, expose) the tares. The owner is symbolic of God. Take note that the difference between the wheat and tare is plainly seen by the mature ones, which worked for the owner. The major difference between wheat and tare is that the tare does not produce grain. Also notice that the owner was not surprised at their news about the tares, nor did he convey a lack of knowledge of their presence. These two facts speak of His foreknowledge of the evil planted seed and the knowledge that they were in His world. His reply found in Matt.13: 29-30 is to allow the wheat to grow along with the tare. God in his infinite wisdom allows children of the kingdom of God to grown among tares, so that we may bear fruit and shine His light in darkness. Thereafter, Jesus tells us that He will send forth His angels and gather out of His kingdom all things that offend and them who do iniquity. The scripture affirms there are ones in His world, which bring offense and do evil. The scripture also gives careful instruction not to uproot the tare in order to prevent the loss of wheat in the field.

Although this parable refers to evil seeds, the ungodly, in the world this same practice is applicable in the Kingdom of God when bringing correction to individual involved in faults or sins in the assembly. Rather than plucking out the individual it serves the body in a greater capacity to offer spiritual counseling and accountability. The results give evidence that *those who adhere* to such discipline benefit greatly. Realizing although the people connected to the person at fault are not tares they have grown next to one, and the root of the tares is wrapped around their root. An undisciplined worker would immediately want to pluck up (expose) the tares, which would remove the good wheat from the soil as well and cause loss of spiritual life. It would be better to continue to nurture the seed of God in the wheat and allow God to ultimately divide the tares from the wheat.

~ *Grow on to Maturity* ~

It is only when we view another part of the body as not a part of "us" that we expose, reveal, or exploit their sin and shame. Ask yourself, would I want someone to expose, reveal, or exploit my past darkest sin? Come on ask yourself, "If this was to *help* the body of Christ would I want my darkest past heart or open sin exploited, revealed, or exposed in the news papers, on the news, in the tabloids or through the Christian information venues?" If I were to take a survey I am sure that a resounding "NO!" would be the overwhelming reply.

With our own short comings in mind I challenge you today to ask God to help you to grow on to maturity, by never again being a trash receptacle for gossip, slander and yes, not to entertain even true unfavorable reports.

Father, we ask you to purge our hearts of the desire to pass, hear or entertain that which is impure. We pray that our hearts would be holy and clean before you. We ask you to help us to be slow to speak, and quick to forgive our brothers and sisters. We ask that you will give us the wisdom to never be used again by the enemy as a tool of division. Thank you that your love is taking deep root in our hearts, causing us to bring forth fruit of long suffering and to display the attributes of love. Thank you for causing our hearts to be joined together as we intercede, bearing the infirmities of the weak, and covering them in prayer. We pray that you will cause us to be one even as You and your Son are one and that the light of your love, illuminating our lives, will brighten the darkened world for Your glory.

~~~~~~~~~~~~~~~~~~ Selah ~~~~~~~~~~~~~~~~~~

Chapter II

The Early Church

~ *Pavements of Suffering* ~

I have often empathized with the hurt, humiliation and shame associated with those who have acquired battle scars for the name of Christ. Some today hold secret scars, hidden in their hearts even from those closest to them, that is only visible when you try to approach them beyond their set comfort zones. Other ministries hold battle scars due to refusing to compromise; thereby, maintaining their integrity and level of anointing. Then there are others who have suffered incredible loss in their finances, family and public reputation. Many have assessed the scars of others and have calculated them as "They missed God," or "They were out of the will of God." This is not necessarily the case.

As it was with the Early Church, we face many attacks. Some are covert and others are overt. It is very important that we refrain from judging others who have gone through such incidents as having spiritual deficits in their lives. In the days to come because of the various methods that will be employed by the enemy to discredit the leaders and the body of Christ, we must sharpen our discernment. It is very crucial that we, as Christians globally, bond together and stand as one, despite persecutions that will arise to undermine the influence and unity of the body of Christ.

I believe the religious freedoms and biblical revelations we enjoy are often taken for granted because people are not fully aware of the sacrificial lives that were given to preserve and advance the gospel of Jesus Christ. When considering the Early Church, we see they endured tremendous suffering for Christ sake. Their example of unity as a result of persecution is written in blood on the pages of time as an example to us today. Various methods of torture were employed during persecutions against the church. As is often the case when studying the accounts of a group of people who have suffered persecution, there are often unwritten, unthinkable, unexplainable, inconceivable atrocities that the world will never know.

The Early Church chronicles of suffering, through historical records, speak of unquestionable loyalty to God. Could it be some how while gazing over the ink filled pages of history we disassociate the reality of the individuals and mentally reduce them to another superficial character as in the nursery rhyme Jack and Jill, who went up the hill to fetch a pail of water? I believe subconsciously, if not by design, we have separated the sufferings and deaths of the historical heroes/heroines from our *real world*.

Perhaps by mentally reducing the persecuted church to mere fictional characters, it alleviates the pain associated with their story. Thereby, we are able to suppress the question that comes to mind - when we see them as people with loved ones like ours, children like ours, having steps ordered by the Lord like ours, a daily confession list like ours, godly callings like ours, having devotion towards God like ours, (come a little closer) and faith that the ultimate persecution will not happen to them like ours — "Could this happen to us?" The underlying question persists, could this same tragedy somehow escape from the pages of time and invade our lives?

It seems as if we, the body of Christ, have subliminally made a list of occurrences that do not happen to spiritually mature Christians. You know of the unspoken Christian referral list that is used as a measuring guideline of things that do not happen to the spiritually elite, if you are in the center of His *perfect will*. The list also consists of the devastating occurrences in the lives of others that one may self-righteously ponder in their heart, "What could they have done to allow a door for the enemy to come in and attack them in such a manner?"

There are a *few* exceptions, which were in the center of His *perfect will*, and endured tremendous sufferings. A portion of the list would include eleven of the disciples, all of the apostles, the Early Church martyrs and nameless others of our day.

Paul spoke very openly of his sufferings in II Corinthians 11:24 recording that he received thirty-nine lashes five times, was beaten with rods three times, stoned once, three times suffered shipwreck, encountering various dangers during his travels, and suffered hunger and thirst.

It seems as if while experiencing the blessings, favor and grace of God upon our lives in the 21st century we have taken our name off the list for the promise found in II Timothy 3:12, stating:

> *"Yea, and all that will live godly in Christ Jesus shall (the word shall makes this a promise) suffer persecution."*

The finest writing skills coupled with intricate details would only give the reader a veiled glimpse of the persecution, suffering, fear, hope, pain, turmoil and emotions experienced by countless martyrs.

~ *Felicitas* ~

Fox's book of Martyrs heralds a historical heroin from the pages of time to our computer world. Fox wrote of Felicitas that she was a married lady, big with child at the time of being apprehended. The unforgivable crime she committed was not denouncing Christ, his teachings, and not worshipping the pagan god. On March 8th, A.D. 205 the day appointed for her execution, she was led to the amphitheater. After being stripped, she was thrown to the bulls. Fox further explains that she was gored dreadfully by the bulls but did not die, so the executioners killed her with a sword.

I have pondered this event while many questions about the life of this precious woman raced through my heart. Where was she born? Who were Falicitas' father and mother? Did she have childhood friends? Did they play tea time and house like children today? How old was she when she submitted her life to God? How did she meet her husband? Did she fall in love at first sight? Did she marry a carpenter? Were they in ministry? Was the child within her the answered prayer of a barren womb? Had she talked to, sang to, named, and dedicated the child while in her womb? What happened to her husband? Whose life did she observe that taught her to have unshakable devotion? How did she prepare to carry out such a noble death? What other God ordained step of obedience did she take in preparation for her final hour of devotion? Was she aware that she too would know the full depth of the meaning of dying for Him? After being captured and before experiencing those last moments of great humiliation what did she say to God? Did she ask him - as I would have - to spare the life of the unborn child? Did she say inwardly when offered a way out by denouncing Christ and His teachings that she would rather lay down her life and the unborn child's? Did she tell God she loved Him unto death before she proved it?

It is when we allow our hearts to ponder the lives of such martyrs that they cease to be only historical characters and become *real* people to us. It escalates our appreciation for their foundation of suffering that has paved the way for the freedoms and revealed biblical truths we now enjoy.

~ *Martyrs for Christ* ~

Our appreciation of Martyrs for Christ adheres to honorably remembering those who were burned at the stake, placed inside entertainment arenas to be eaten by ravenous beasts, decapitated, torn asunder and crucified. There were also many that were used maliciously for entertainment because of their faith and belief in the Lord Jesus Christ.

Fox's Book of Martyrs gives other historical accounts where early Christians were used as scapegoats for the cruel acts of Nero, the sixth emperor of Rome. It is recorded that after Nero gave the order to set the city of Rome ablaze, that upon hearing of the anger of the citizens he quickly placed the blame upon Christians (A.D. 64). This deceitful act gave way to a tolerance level of Christian persecution not previously witnessed.

The demonic influence upon Nero's mind brought about hideous acts such as sewing Christians inside of bloody animal skins and allowing dogs to gnaw at the remains of the beast until the Christians died. He also had shirts soaked in wax and after dressing the Christians in this torturous fashion, tied them to axletrees and mercilessly set them on fire to give light to his garden. Go ahead ask the questions did they have wives, husbands, parents, children, followers, and a reason to live?

Another ruler, Domitian, ordered the entire lineage of David to be put to death. It was during his leadership that the disciple John was boiled in oil and banished to the Isle Patmos.

During the Roman rule of Adrian, about 10,000 Christians were martyred. In Mount Ararat, Christians were crucified with crowns of thorns upon their head, and speared in their side as a mockery of the death of Christ.

Cruelties of Marcus Aurelius (A.D. 161) include scourging to the extent of the martyrs sinews and veins becoming openly visible; thereafter, they were destroyed by conscienceless acts.

Another martyr, Bishop Polycarp of Smyrna after feeding his captors requested an hour of prayer. This granted request to spend one of his last earthly hours in an intimate sweet hour of fervent prayer caused the guards with great repentance of heart to carry him before the proconsul where he was offered a release from imminent death if he would denounce Jesus Christ. The Bishop's reply was, "Eighty and six years have I served Him, and He never once wronged me; how then shall I blaspheme my King, Who hath saved me?" He then being condemned, and sentenced to burn, assured his executioners that if he was tied to the stake rather than nailed, as was the custom, that he would not remove himself. When the blaze was set to the debris beneath him, rather than consuming him the flame became a circle round about him. Then the executioners were ordered to pierce him with a sword. This fatal wound served as a bridge rendering him absent from the body, but present with the LORD! Remember that this happened on this side of Calvary's cross.

Justin, a great philosopher and universal scholar, also answered the call of ultimate loyalty. To his credit are writings to the Gentiles as well as to the Jews. His search for truth brought him to the TRUTH that Jesus Christ is the Son of God, sent to earth to redeem man from sin. It is this conviction that prompted him to open a school teaching others, who later became great men used by God mightily. Justin wrote many epistles to the Gentiles telling them of Jesus Christ. He also used his gift of writing as a tool to reach the Jews in an attempt to convince them of the truth of Jesus Christ. Inevitably Justin, along with six other of his companions, became martyrs because of the truths they shared. When captured, they too were offered freedom if they would sacrifice to pagan idols and denounce Christ and His teachings. Upon refusal, they were scourged and beheaded.

The image of the early Christians gleaning strength from each other; linking their bodies together to form human chains and encouraging one another to keep the faith until death is engraved in my spirit. This is an example of how we should bind ourselves together in the love of God, encouraging one another to keep the faith as we impart the strength required to complete the purpose of God in the earth.

It is easy to see that the Early Church Christians possessed a strong resilience intertwined with faith. Their faith in Christ was worth sacrificing everything, including their lives. Their loyalty and faith gave them the strength to face the lion's den, and go before the Roman rulers without compromising their beliefs that Jesus is the Son of God. These heroes/heroines of faith were not secret service under cover closet Christians. They indeed were courageous followers of Christ. The disciples of Jesus were stoned, ran out of towns, imprisoned, tortured, beaten, beheaded, crucified upside down and endured great persecutions for the name of Christ.

~ *Today's Persecuted Church* ~

It is important in the days ahead we remember one vital saying of Jesus when his mother and brother stood without inquiring of Him and those surrounding Him approached saying your mother and brother are asking for you. Jesus replied "Who is my mother? Who is my brother? But those who do the will of my father." While Jesus is accomplishing the will of the Father He takes out the time to teach his disciplined ones that his family is those who pursue God.

Being we, as Christians are all one body, we are a part of the Early Church and the Early Church is a part of the present church age. The bloodstained seeds of endurance sown into the earth by the Early Church have brought forth fruit, which has produced, boundless harvest for the furtherance of the gospel and unity.

The church today is constantly taking new ground and utilizing new technologies, methods and procedures, reaping a greater harvest than ever experienced to date. We, the end-time portion of the body of Christ, are the benefactors of the sufferings endured by the Early Church. The fruit of our inheritance is the ability to spread the Gospel of Jesus Christ to the uttermost parts of the earth, which is an eternal testimony that the Early Church martyrs to our present day martyrs have not died in vain.

It is amazing how all of the different parts of the Early Church were tied together. Regardless of which group of Christians was instrumental in their conversions, their hearts and lives were woven together because of ENORMOUS persecutions.

I was given the opportunity through friends of ours to meet two pastors who had suffered greatly because they are carriers of the gospel. Due to the persecution that they face on a daily basis they will remain anonymous. One of the pastors was from India and the other one was from another country in Asia, Vietnam.

The pastor from India and his staff, along with our friends, have been used greatly by God to bring the gospel of Jesus Christ to unreached areas in India. They have walked endless miles, endured deplorable living conditions, working with very exiguous resources, and in most cases without adequate resources. Their buildings and equipment have been vandalized too many times to tell. They too, know what it is to be taken away from their families, imprisoned and labeled as "disturbing the peace" because they were preaching the gospel.

The pastor from Vietnam has also endured great persecution. The underground church in parts of Asia is restricted from holding any gatherings. When they meet for service their praise and worship is very different from ours. The worship services are conducted with the knowledge that at any given moment their services may be interrupted and their leaders may be slain or taken to prison. However, they have adopted the "no problem" attitude. When faced with prison their response is "no problem" the Lord is sending me into the prison ministry. When faced with death their response is "no problem" and thank you very much, for to be absent from the body is to be present with the LORD!

The leaders of the churches have been imprisoned numerous lengthy times. It is very different from America in that they, like Jesus, have to tell those who are healed through their ministry go and tell no one, because they are meeting and ministering the gospel *illegally.*

It is so amazing that without any public advertisement they are experiencing staggering church growth. The growth of the church in Asia is so phenomenal that they are constantly training new leaders and forming new small home church groups to accommodate the needs of the people.

Upon individually asking both pastors what they saw as the greatest tool in uniting the church, they both responded, *persecution.* Both pastors recalled incidents of how the church multiplied greatly as they or the various leaders were imprisoned, or their homes were destroyed, or when individuals of their church lost their lives because of the gospel of Jesus Christ. Even though I asked both men the same question at different times the answer was the same, and the accounts of church growth due to persecution was also consistent.

During a meeting one of the leaders from Asia voiced this request "Do not pray that the persecution stops, but pray that we will see His glory." How many people do you know who have been imprisoned, assaulted, having the property that they've worked for years to acquire confiscated, their name placed on a black list, in some cases not able to meet publicly, and their every move watched who are yet saying "Do not pray that the persecution stops but pray that we will see His glory"? They are few and far between.

It is people like this that I consider great in the kingdom of God. The marked qualities shared among the individuals, are true humility and the heart of a servant. Although these individuals have multiplied thousand of members it is hard to perform any duties for them. They are always searching for a way to serve others.

Another leader of the underground church testified that during the years her husband was incarcerated, for preaching the gospel, she carried on the work that the Lord had commissioned them to do. Guess what was her number one prayer request? No, it was not Lord release my husband. No, it was not keep him safe. No, it was not Lord you know since he is in there because of you; you owe me everything I need to survive. You will never guess it. She and many others continued the prayer, initiated by their imprisoned leader, every day for five years, "Lord, show us your glory."

She further stated that her father had given his life for the gospel's sake. She said after her father died and her husband was imprisoned she continued to regard her life not as her own, but stated if she had two lives she would give both of them for God. I don't know about you but upon hearing her devotion to God I said, like the older saints, "Lord save me again." That's the kind of devotion I admire. There are some people in life, who cross your path, that give flesh to the words written by the Apostle Paul:

"For I reckon that the sufferings of this present time are not worthy to be compared with the glory which shall be revealed in us." (Romans 8:18)

Today there are yet seventy-eight nations with some form of Christian persecution. Whether reading an article or talking with individuals who are suffering various forms of persecution, there remains one common thread, all forms of persecution produced unity among the groups of Christians.

~ *God's Check and Balance System* ~

Fox's book of Martyrs provides a good example of unity during persecution when Maximinus ruled. During the leadership of Maximinus, Christians were executed without trials, and were buried in heaps of fifty to sixty bodies in a pit. During such studies of persecution, you will see repeatedly where the church grew, walking in love and unity with each other. Notice that in times of peace or lack of persecution, the church continued to grow; however, divisions and erroneous teachings crept in among the people of God.

After the death of Maximinus A.D. 238 and during the time of his successor Gordian, and his successor Phillip's reign, the church experienced more than 10 years of freedom from reported persecution. The pagan temples experienced minimal support and the church prospered. It is also reported that as they enjoyed freedom from persecution, they became full of pride because of their newly found growth. Divisions became rampant and erroneous teachings and doctrines infiltrated the church. It is sad to say, the same pattern continues today.

It is to be noted that whenever the church divided, erroneous teachings also accompanied the divisions. God has set in place a check and balance system in His body. We absolutely need each other. When the body of Christ functions together, the spoken and unspoken accountability unto one another produces a spiritual check and balance system or vaccine, which serves as a form of resistance or immunization against erroneous doctrines and teachings.

I have noticed when leaders from different parts of the body are in covenant relationships, which includes some form of spiritual fellowship and accountability, the people they serve benefit greatly by possessing an unusual spiritual balance. You will find among them groups of believers having a unique appreciation for other expressions of the body of Christ.

As is the case with most immunization measures, there are a few instances where the disease will persist, and the body contacts the illness. As is the case with a natural disease, the effects are minimized because of the vaccination. As a general rule, erroneous doctrines will not be among those who have this check and balance system. The name of their church or leader will not be mentioned during the worship service more than the name of the Lord, nor strange "spiritual" practices, nor attacks against another part of the body.

This is the type of balance the early-persecuted church possessed. On a large scale they did not allow the origins of their groups to serve as a tool of division. When the different groups of believers gathered, the main question was not which home prayer meeting the new converts would attend, and it is certain that doctrinal issues were not the major *issue*.

Would it be presumptuous to assume none of the Early Church believers, having received the gospel through the preaching of John the Baptist or his disciples, asked others who were converted through the teachings of Jesus' disciples doctrinal views while being tortured, stoned, burned, beaten, boiled in oil, having to watch their children die, or being thrown into arenas for ravenous beasts to devour?

Unity

Furthermore, I seriously doubt if while in death arenas they decided to divide the area into sections saying: "Hear ye! Hear ye! Every one who believes that once you are saved you are always saved, you have been assigned to the first quarter of the arena. All of those who believe that you are not saved if you are not water baptized, the second quarter of the arena is reserved for you. Oh yes, those of you who are in ministry with no accountability the third quarter is yours to run about freely. Finally if you believe there is no rapture (taking away) of the righteous, the fourth quarter is for you." Now that all of the Christians who are to be devoured are separated into the various belief sections, here come the lions. Guess what? The lions see all of the prisoners for what they are, *DINNER*!

The beast is not preoccupied with which group you are a part of, his entire purpose is to consume and utterly destroy. One may say in their heart that it is ridiculous to think that Christians would ponder such thoughts while their enemy is waiting for an opportunity to devour them. I concur with you; however, this could be viewed as the current state of the body of Christ. There are many challenges of division among us, and the devourer is yet seeking whom he may devour.

I am aware that the church (on a large scale) may not see herself in this light, but we are in a spiritual arena where the enemy desires to devour us and we are segregated in our various belief zones because of minor differences. I am persuaded if we really could discern the spiritual ravenous beasts of carnality, sexual sins, improper use of church funds, lack of church leadership, deficits of loyalty, spiritual brokenness, legal persecutions, divisions within, divisions without, prayerlessness, lack of consecration, rating success by numbers rather than fulfilling the will of God, lethargy, strife, contention, divorce, comparing ourselves among ourselves, scarcity of spiritual fathers thereby rampant undisciplined behavior, the love of money, pride, slothfulness, racial prejudice, denominational prejudice, and numerous other spiritual devouring beasts we would not be divided on temporal issues. It is true if we really could see ourselves in an arena where beasts are lurking to devour the body of Christ; such divisions would not exist.

~ *Grounds of Division* ~

Many grounds of division persist, such as:

Should we observe the Sabbath on Saturday or Sunday?
Should water baptism be in the name of the Father, Son and Holy Ghost or in Jesus' Name?
Is tithing for the New Testament Church?
Are you saved before or after baptism?
Must one have the indwelling of the Holy Spirit with the evidence of speaking in tongues to have eternal life?
Are spiritual tongues essential for victorious living?
Is the Holy Spirit received when you receive Jesus as your Lord and Savior or as a separate experience?
Is the rapture scriptural?
Is healing for this present time?
Is God the Father, Son, and Holy Ghost one person or one manifested as the Trinity, or three separate persons?
If once saved are we eternally secure?

All of these questions and countless others have served as differences on which to base various divisions in the body of Christ. The list of differences could stretch on and on forever. However, I like the call of maturity, heard through the ages in Hebrews 6:1-2:

> *1 Therefore leaving the principles of the doctrine of Christ, let us go on unto perfection; not laying*

> *again the foundation of repentance from dead works, and of faith toward God,*
>
> *2 Of the doctrine of baptisms, and of laying on of hands, and of resurrection of the dead, and of eternal judgment.*

Although all of the aforementioned issues are important, they are on a level that is the first principle of the oracles of God (Hebrews 5:12). God at this hour is calling His people to stand on the foundation He has established through the pastors, prophets, evangelists, apostles, and teachers and go on unto perfection.

~ *The Perfecting of the Saints* ~

If we iron out all of the doctrinal differences between each group of believers, it would be the equivalent of forever laying a foundation or forever learning and never coming into the meat of the truth. It is like building a house and never deciding that the foundation is complete. When this occurs the real building that the architect had in mind is never realized.

No one ever drives by the foundation of a building construction site and say "Oh my, I would love to see what is inside that marvelous foundation. I love the way the light gently encompasses the grass patched heaps of dirt surrounding the foundation. Such brilliant architectural skills used to display the glory of that hole!" No! If we make the foundations (our various doctrines and beliefs) a shrine we worship, refusing to build onward to perfecting our love for the entire body of Christ, we will not fully utilize the spiritual architectural gifting of the apostles, prophets, evangelists, pastors, and teachers. Ephesians 4:11-16 states:

11 And He gave some, apostles; and some, prophets; and some, evangelists; and some, pastors and teachers;
12 For the perfecting of the saints, for the work of the ministry, for the edifying of the body of Christ:
13 Till we all come in the unity of the faith, and of the knowledge of the Son of God, unto a perfect man, unto the measure of the stature of the fullness of Christ:
14 That we henceforth be no more children, tossed to and fro, and carried about with every wind of doctrine, by the sleight of men, and cunning craftiness, whereby they lie in wait to deceive;
15 But speaking the truth in love, may grow up into him in all things, which is the head, even Christ:
16 From whom the whole body fitly joined together and compacted by that which every joint supplieth, according to the effectual working in the measure of every part, maketh increase of the body unto the edifying of itself in love.

The five fold ministries are gifted to add to the foundation in turn produce the completion of the building project, the perfecting of the saints for the work of the ministry, the unity of the faith, the knowledge of the Son of God, bringing about maturity, speaking truth in love, causing the body to be fitly joined together, and edifying itself in love.

I believe the reason why we are not seeing more perfected (matured) saints is because we, the body, have reduced the five-fold perfecting ministry gifts to perpetual foundation layers. So the scenario persists that on a large scale the reservoir of perfecting truths lies untapped in our apostles, prophets, evangelist, pastors and teachers. Their time is occupied primarily by the fleshly appetites of Christians crying for the foundational milk of repentance from dead works, sins and trespasses, and of faith toward God; such cries as, "Pastor tell me again why I should know beyond a shadow of a doubt that God is real and working on my behalf." Also their time is occupied with teachings of the doctrine of baptisms, and of laying on of hands, and of the resurrection of the dead, and of eternal judgment. Paul lists the issues that so many have majored in, as foundation truths.

There is a perfecting word from the architect, our God the creator, planted in the womb of our apostles, prophets, evangelists, pastors, and teachers that has reached maturity. However, there is a scarcity of believers that are able to produce milk that would nourish the delivered word until it comes to a matured state in their life. It is when the Word has matured in the lives of believers that it nourishes our communities, turns the hearts of our teens, transforms the lives of our loved ones, brings justice to our judicial system, purifies our legislation, turns our nation's heart back to God, takes the light of the gospel to every creature, and presents unto Him a bride without spot, wrinkle, blemish or any such thing, walking in unity and love.

~ *A Word from the Lord* ~

Without unity in the body of Christ we are destined to play out the role of ever learning and never coming into the knowledge of the truth. The aforementioned issues and many others have served as grounds for division in the body of Christ. At this hour God is erasing the denominational segregated lines from our hearts. While our world is experiencing devastation and challenges not known to our nation before, God is knitting our hearts together.

On September 11, 2001 the most hideous acts of terrorism on the soil of the United States of America occurred. The destruction of the Twin Towers brought our nation to its knees.

That day, for a moment in time, we ceased to be rich, poor, Black, White, Protestant, Catholic, Republican, Democrat or Independent. We were all American's with bleeding hearts. We gained a new appreciation for our country and the freedoms we enjoy and have often taken for granted. After that day we said the pledge of allegiance with a new depth of heart. We all shed tears filled with plea as we sang God Bless America. The change in our world was seen for months to follow as people greeted strangers while passing in the streets with great sincerity of heart. The brief greetings were laced with the knowledge that the world, we all had known before, was forever changed.

While listening to programs of prophecy teachers I have heard many times that the future of our country, America, is not specifically stated in the Bible. During a service I attended in 1998 the aforementioned statement was made and God spoke to me saying that He was **allowing America an opportunity to prophetically write her own future through her actions**. He reminded me of how this nation was founded by people with hearts in pursuit of Him. He further reminded me that this nation has sent missionaries across the world for Him and He has not forgotten America's labor of love.

After the attacks in New York, the words that the Lord spoke to me regarding America was that in past years our nation had taken a moral route that would not bring us to His desired end. Also, He had placed our country in a political position to be a blessing to Israel and we had made some decisions that were not in Israel's favor. He went on to say that the desire of the enemy was to bring devastation far beyond anything we could imagine but He held us in His hand and many lives were spared.

It was not His will that this act of terror would occur, but He has chosen to use it for His purpose. Therefore, prior to September 11, 2001, He allowed key people to occupy strategic offices to shoulder and direct our country in both political and spiritual arenas. That is why there was such a war in the spirit regarding political and spiritual leadership. It was designed to separate us in every area of our country and to place others, not designated for this hour, in key governmental and spiritual leadership at our most crucial hour. However, He held us in his hand and brought promotion according to His will and purpose.

Because of His love for America He has not only set before our country life and death with the prompting to choose life, He has also turned our nation towards the path that will ensure His blessing. He has in fact given us another opportunity to be a blessing to Israel so that His blessing and grace will be upon our nation to withstand that, which is to come. He has also turned the hearts and minds of our country back towards Him.

I admonish you to not slack in prayer for the leaders of our nation, because their actions are prophesying our nation's future. I also plead that you would walk holy before the Lord (remembering God's challenge to find 10 righteous in Sodom and Gomorrah). So, finally the Lord is saying to this nation, even as He said unto Israel:

If my people, which are called by my name, shall humble themselves, and pray, and seek my face, and turn from their wicked ways; then will I hear from heaven, and will forgive their sin, and will heal their land. (II Chronicles 7:14)

~ *Win the Lost* ~

The cry of our lost world has reached a heart wrenching level that removes any former guideline or boundaries of how to reach the lost. We must now reach them with the same urgency that one would display if a person were in a burning building. "By any means necessary!"

It is imperative we eliminate our doctrinal segregated belief zones, so we may adopt weapons and armor that other portions of the body have proven to be victorious against the enemy.

I look for the day that we, as the Early Church did, would tie ourselves to one another with that one common thread, seen prophetically prior to the death of Christ, by the scarlet in the high priest garment, and by the red rope Rahab used to signal the army of Israel to spare her household's life. In both instances it foreshadows the blood of Jesus that now flows through our spiritual veins, tying us together. It is when we see ourselves through His shed blood we will experience the greatest victories the body of Christ has ever known.

This is the hour that was prophesied of old saying, *"And it shall come to pass in the last days, saith God, I will pour out my spirit upon all flesh..."* The glory of the Lord shall cover the earth as the waters cover the sea. People from every nation, tribe and tongue shall speak forth His excellent praise, bringing people to repentance from the highest levels of authority through out the land as we unify ourselves under His command and march as a UNITED ARMY.

~~~~~~~~~~~~~~~~~ Selah ~~~~~~~~~~~~~~~~~

Chapter III

David

~ A Father's Plea ~

David, by the divine inspiration of God, has called our attention to the importance of unity. Some say that Psalm 133 was written when the tribes collectively made David their king. Others say that this psalm was written to his sons to evoke a sense of unity among them. Many thoughts about unity have evolved from this psalm; however, the scenario of a father attempting to convey the natural intertwined with the spiritual beauty of unity is dear to my heart.

Throughout the ages, parents across the globe have given several universal commands to their children. Don't fight with your brother/sister. Love one another. Don't mistreat your brother/sister. You two work it out because you are family. Watch out for your brother/sister. The father's heart in David was no different than a parent of our day. Within David's appeal for unity is mirrored a facet of God the Father's appeal for unity.

> *Psalms 133:1* **Behold, how good and how pleasant it is for brethren to dwell together in unity!**

> *2 It is like the precious ointment upon the head, that ran down upon the beard, even Aaron's beard: that went down to the skirts of his garments;*
> *3 As the dew of Hermon, and as the dew that descended upon the mountains of Zion: for there the LORD commanded the blessing, even life for evermore.*

As was the culture of his day, various women conceived David's sons. There are many aspects contributing to the character of David's sons. For example, the culture; the fact they were all children of the king; therefore princes, their mother's culture and character, and other outside influences all played a great part in the sculpture of their character. It is also quite common to find traits of the parents planted deep inside a child's mannerism, character, and beliefs.

I Chronicles 3 list David's sons.

> *1 Now these were the sons of David, which were born unto him in Hebron; the firstborn Amnon, of Ahinoam the Jezreelitess; the second Daniel, of Abigail the Carmelitess:*
> *2 The third, Absalom the son of Maachah the daughter of Talmai king of Geshur: the fourth, Adonijah the son of Haggith:*
> *3 The fifth, Shephatiah of Abital: the sixth, Ithream by Eglah his wife.*
> *4 These six were born unto him in Hebron; and there he reigned seven years and six months: and in Jerusalem he reigned thirty-and three years.*
> *5 And these were born unto him in Jerusalem; Shimea, and Shobab, and Nathan, and Solomon, four, of Bathshua the daughter of Ammiel:*
> *6 Ibhar also, and Elishama, and Eliphelet,*
> *7 And Nogah, and Nepheg, and Japhia,*

> *8 And Elishama, and Eliada, and Eliphelet, nine.*
> *9 These were all the sons of David, beside the sons of the concubines, and Tamar their sister.*

It is very important that we examine the character of David to understand the behavior of his sons.

The definition of David's name is *beloved*. David's name, in Hebrew, comes from the word meaning *to boil*. David, a man after the heart of God, who acquired the heart of a shepherd while tending his father's sheep, pursued God relentlessly. David the man, who danced, worshipping before the Lord with uninhibited praise and thanksgiving in the face of disfavor, is also the same man who demonstrated uncompromising loyalty and restraint toward God's anointed, King Saul, while fleeing for his life. No wonder he was affectionately called beloved.

Nevertheless, he is also the man who after God elevated him to king and gave him more than he could ever ask or think, coveted the wife of his loyal servant, Uriah. Thereafter, he defiled her, then plotted and deceived, and ultimately choreographed Uriah's demise.

In every one of our lives there is a point we will come to, if we choose to fulfill the destiny of God for our lives that embodies what it means to boil. It is in that hour everything not dealt with, crucified, and submitted unto Him will surface due to life's boiling tests and trials. Furthermore, if God allows what has surfaced will also come to an open shame.

The part of David's character that surfaced when his kingly temptations came to the place of boiling arose at a very crucial historical moment that has and will be remembered throughout the ages. David had passed the initial place of boiling when he faced his priestly temptation by not retreating when facing the lion, bear and Goliath. David was also very valiant passing the test of his princely anointing, leading Saul's army killing his ten thousands, and later not prematurely over throwing Saul's authority.

It is the kingly hour we often fail to prepare for. It is the hour we are submerged in blessings and favor that yes men with numbed convictions, lacking the backbone and courage to speak a word for God, surround us. That is the time that we must be most sensitive to the voice of the Lord, so that we will not find ourselves on the threshold of error and disobedience. It is in that hour that integrity must be woven into the very fiber of our beings. This is the time the fabric of your life is labeled through past character building test and trials.

Through the ages people small and great have humbled themselves, fasted, prayed, sought council and walked softly in the presence of the Lord refusing to touch that which belongs to God. The real test is after experiencing success and recognition at the height of the princely anointing, and while enjoying the blessings of God that human error has caused many to fail in preparation for the kingly level of temptations.

The timing of the kingly anointing is very peculiar. It is often when your spiritual father has been carried away perhaps in a chariot, like Elisha, while tossing you his double portion mantle that the kingly anointing occurs. Or perhaps in the case of Joshua, your mentor has been told to go to a mountain and die, leaving you to guide millions across the Jordan without prior foot prints that you shed like a snake-skin the princely anointing and He clothes you with the kingly anointing. You are living your dream and your nightmare at the same time. You are looked upon as a benchmark but you are trying to remember exactly what level you must maintain to retain the benchmark. You kneel to pray and you are immediately in the presence of the Lord hearing daily instructions. You want to offer the sacrifice of praise but the weight of your call causes you to lay prostrate with groaning which can not be uttered. In His presence you are mindful of His awesome power on your behalf, your new garment of responsibility, and your frailty without Him. Your best friend, in David's case Jonathan, has gone off the scene and you are encompassed with new faces, learning to trust again. It is then that you are faced with the test, which will serve like a family crest, identifying to the world the ministry of God upon your life.

Have you ever thought about the guidance Saul could have imparted unto David? Saul, like most other leaders possessed the ability to discern the call of God upon David's life; however, jealousy prevented him from mentoring David to excel his reign.

One mark of a true leader is the ability to equip, train and develop those they serve to excel their works. This is why when a good leader leaves for a short period of time; the area of ministry the pastor has entrusted to their care does not become disassembled. Each department of ministry should function as smoothly as if the leader were there. This of course requires one to be secure in who and what they are, because human nature is to want people to depend upon you to the point that there is something major lacking if you are not there. Jesus was so secure in his personal calling, and in the ministry which he imparted to his disciples that he declared "Greater works shall you do".

Although David did not have a noted human mentor, he excelled his predecessor. We will never know if the deposit of a true mentor could have prevented David from failing his greatest test. Notice in David's history, he has many acts of loyalty, victory and worship towards God, but his misuse of kingly authority marred his reputation and remains forever a part of his historical family crest.

After David's sin with Bathsheba, he ruled many more years, completing his forty year reign. David gathered an enormous amount of material for the temple of God and defeated the enemies of Israel, but his legacy suffered greatly because he did not pass the temptation that was woven with covetousness, deceit and lust for Bathsheba.

~ *David's Sons* ~

Considering David's struggles, we are better equipped to identify the devices of the enemy that came against his seed. Ahinoam the Jezreelitess birthed David's first son Amnon. He is infamous for his transgression against his sister Tamar. The meaning of the name Amnon is *faithful and true tutor*. His mother's name Ahinoam is defined as *brother of pleasantness, brother of grace*.

There are no biblical accounts of good or evil doings of Amnon until he came to a point in his life where his lack of disciplined emotions reduced him from being a faithful and true tutor to sitting in the counsel of the ungodly. It was upon receiving the evil seed planted by his cousin Jonadab, that he rejected his true inherited nature of a brother of pleasantness accompanied with grace and was made a victim of the same sin that caused his father to ensure the death of Uriah, the Hittite.

There was much redemptive strength available to Amnon. In biblical times, names were often given as a prophetic expression of the perceived nature of an individual. It was not uncommon to witness the defining character of a person's name projected throughout their life. This being the case, Amnon having a nurturer whose name defined a brother of pleasantness and grace was from birth around the character and discipline required for passing the greatest test of his life. Furthermore, his mother also being a Jezreelitess came from a place that God had and would use to establish natural and spiritual grounds of victory.

Various theologians give three to five geographical locations of cities named Jezreel. One city of Jezreel is found in the hill country of Judah, near Jokdeam and Zanoa. It is

Unity

assumed that the present day Khirbet Terrama on the plain of Debleh is the location where Amnon's mother was born. Another city of Jezreel is found in Northern Israel on a plain 56 miles north of Jerusalem in the territory of Issachar belonging to the tribe of Manasseh. Whether referring to the given birth place of Amnon's mother or to one of the other locations the implications remain the same. Jezreel is a land where God established victories over oppressing forces.

Judges the sixth chapter gives the account where Israel is delivered into the hands of Midian because of disobedience. They were driven out of their land by the Midianites, and lived in caves and mountains for seven years. Thereafter, the children of Israel cried unto the Lord and He forgave them and brought great deliverance in Jezreel by the hand of Gideon against the Midianites and Amalekites (Judges 7). Another deliverance is seen later where Jehu brings about the death of Jezebel, who orchestrated the death of the prophets and opened the spiritual doors of whoredoms (idolatry) and witchcraft (rebellion) among the people (Joshua 19:18).

If Amnon had utilized the God given redemptive strengths available to him, he would have left a legacy throughout history as a faithful and true tutor, an outstanding brother of pleasantness, loyal and beloved of God, and having lived a victorious life over the sexual oppression that served as an assassin of his destiny.

David's second son is Daniel. His name means *like his father*. Abigail the Carmelitess is his mother. The meaning of Abigail's name is *my father is my joy*. Found in the character of Daniel's nurturer Abigail is wisdom, intercession, and prophecy. This is seen very vividly when David (beloved of God) is running for his life from Saul. David was in the wilderness when he sent 10 men to Nabal, a rich man in Carmel, to request provision for the 600 men who were with him. Upon Nabal's brutal refusal to give David and his men any provisions, he ordered 400 of his men to gather their swords and follow him to Nabal's home.

Meanwhile one of Nabal's servants told Abigail, who was Nabal's wife, David's men had served as a wall of protection both night and day during the time they were tending sheep in the wilderness and did not allow any harm to come upon them.

In the following brief moment of history Daniel's nurturer demonstrates the wisdom of God, interceding for the life of those in her household, and speaks prophetically to the king within David.

> *I Samuel 25:21 Now David had said, Surely in vain have I kept all that this fellow hath in the wilderness, so that nothing was missed of all that pertained unto him: and he hath requited me evil for good.*
>
> *22 So and more also do God unto the enemies of David, if I leave of all that pertain to him by the morning light any that pisseth against the wall.*
>
> *23 And when Abigail saw David, she hasted, and lighted off the ass, and fell before David on her face, and bowed herself to the ground,*
>
> *24 And fell at his feet, and said, Upon me, my lord, upon me let this iniquity be: and let thine handmaid, I pray thee, speak in thine audience, and hear the words of thine handmaid.*
>
> *25 Let not my lord, I pray thee, regard this man of Belial, even Nabal: for as his name is, so is he; Nabal is his name, and folly is with him: but I thine handmaid saw not the young men of my lord, whom thou didst send.*
>
> *26 Now therefore, my lord, as the LORD liveth, and as thy soul liveth, seeing the LORD hath withholden thee from coming to shed blood, and from avenging thyself with thine own hand, now let*

> *thine enemies, and they that seek evil to my lord, be as Nabal.*
> *27 And now this blessing which thine handmaid hath brought unto my lord, let it even be given unto the young men that follow my lord. (She brought provision for him and his followers.)*
> *28 I pray thee, forgive the trespass of thine handmaid: (she prophesied) for the LORD will certainly make my lord a sure house; because my lord fighteth the battles of the LORD, and evil hath not been found in thee all thy days.*
> *29 Yet a man is risen to pursue thee, and to seek thy soul: but the soul of my lord shall be bound in the bundle of life with the LORD thy God; and the souls of thine enemies, them shall he sling out, as out of the middle of a sling.*
> *30 And it shall come to pass, when the LORD shall have done to my lord according to all the good that he hath spoken concerning thee, and shall have appointed thee ruler over Israel;*
> *31 That this shall be no grief unto thee, nor offense of heart unto my lord, either that thou hast shed blood causeless, or that my lord hath avenged himself: but when the LORD shall have dealt well with my lord, then remember thine handmaid.*

Through wisdom, prophesy, and intercession David's anger was turned away.

Nabal soon dies and David marries his widow Abigail. Daniel is the product of that union.

Considering Daniel had the nurturing of a mother possessing wisdom, the spirit of prophesy, the heart of an intercessor coupled with the attributes of his father being beloved of God, and *like his father* he was equipped for kingdom success.

David's third son is Absalom. The meaning of Absalom's name is *my father is peace*. Maachah, meaning *oppression*, the daughter of the King of Geshur, Talmai, meaning *profit* (to gain advantage) *of the people*, married David. The marriage of a King and a princess was often the method to secure an alliance with another kingdom. Most theologians believe that this marriage was a political strategy to secure an alliance north of Judah. Absalom is the product of this marriage.

Absalom is remembered for killing his brother Amnon for defiling his sister Tamar. Absalom took his sister into his home, serving as a covering for her, and waited two years holding hate in his heart before he avenged her by killing Amnon. Thereafter, he fled to his grandfather's kingdom in Geshur and dwelt there for three years.

Five years of his life was consumed and his future was ultimately destroyed because of unforgiveness. An unforgiving heart is an incubation tomb that produces rebellion, strife, and lawlessness. The same demon Absalom tried to subdue through the flesh by killing Amnon possessed him when he listened to the ungodly counsel of Ahithophel and took his father's concubines and lay with them in the sight of all Israel.

Considering Absalom's name, it would have been to his advantage to seek the council of his father. We will never know if David's intervention would have brought about a peaceful end to the spirit of offense and revenge that Absalom held against Amnon. Nor will we ever know if David's intervention would have fostered a parental respect serving as a deterrent to Absalom's later actions against himself.

Absalom's life took on the meaning of his maternal nurturer, Maachah and Talmai; he became the definition of oppression and the verb intransitive meaning of profit of the people. Absalom thereby, oppressed his father and caused the people who were originally for David's kingdom to

Unity

work for his profit and self-gain. Absalom's heart of hatred, lawlessness, disloyalty, and murder was not quenched upon the demise of Amnon. He later proves that rebellion has no loyalty to anyone when he attempts to take the kingdom from his father's aged hands.

David's marriage to Maachah also addresses the political union and relationships outside of the kingdom of God. Beware of intimately linking outside of the kingdom of God with people, businesses, legal entities, and others for protection emotionally, financially, legally, or otherwise. There are times that God will allow you to make friends with mammon. Beware not to marry (intimately link) them into your ministry, because they will produce a seed that will rise up to take out of your aged (matured ministry) hands the portion of the kingdom that God has purposed for you and your seed to guard, multiply and keep.

Adonijah, meaning *my lord is Jehovah*, is David's fourth son, who later poses as a rival against Solomon for the throne. His mother is Haggith, meaning *festive*. Imagine the delight of David if Adonijah had perceived his rightful purpose of being born for such a time to birth into his father's kingdom a people who know their God serving Him with festive joy. However, Adonijah had a character flaw that marred him and later was instrumental in bringing about his death. Adonijah always wanted what was purposed for another. His last request for his father David's virgin wife, Abishag the Shunammite, caused Solomon to order his death.

Notice Solomon did not put him to death for what he did to take the kingdom from his hands, but when Adonijah proved again to be disloyal to his father's memory, Solomon ordered his death.

If people are not loyal to their righteous nurturer know that being loyal to you will also be a *challenge*. It would be wise of you to closely monitor and evaluate their intimate (covenant) relationship with you until the seed of loyalty is conceived in them and brings forth fruit.

Let's make it a little more direct. If your new spiritual partner has received nurturing from a honorable church, or minister with whom they had a covenant relationship (i.e. they were a member that was taken into the ministry leader's confidence, an armor bearer, or a close friend of the ministry) and the report that comes out of their mouth is disloyal, revealing character flaws and private matters know that unless they develop their character in this area, they will also be disloyal to you. Therefore, it is questionable whether or not it is wisdom to receive that disgruntled member as your confidant.

Shephatiah, meaning *Jehovah has judged*, is David's fifth son. His mother's name is Abital, meaning *my father is dew*. Perhaps dwelling in this son was the judgments of the Lord, which are true and righteous all together; more to be desired are they than gold. It is when Jehovah judges that he causes the barren, desolate, dry places of your life to be refreshed by the father's dew, bringing new life to every dead situation.

Eglah, meaning *heifer* is the nurturer of Ithream, meaning *furrowed,* David's sixth son. A heifer is a young unmated cow. Every portion of the cow is of use to man. Even the refuse from their bodies is used to fertilize and nurture the ground so it may reproduce. Webster's dictionary defines furrowed as a trench made by a plough. This is the type of person who is not married to the world and is walking in the earth as betrothed to God. When a person's life defines what is plowed, they are tender before God and can be used as a path for the life giving water (Spirit) of God to flow in and through, and every experience that comprises their life's story is of use to the Master to make fertile soil, nurture, and bring forth life yielding substance.

Bathsheba is the nurturer of the following four sons of David. Shimea, meaning *the hearing prayer*, is David's seventh son.

Shobab, *meaning apostate* (Webster - one who renounces his religion or his party. -a. False; traitorous), is David's eighth son.

Nathan, who is named in the genealogy of Mary (Luke 3:31), is David's ninth son.

Solomon, meaning *peace,* also called Jedediah, is David's successor to the throne. He is greatly known for the wisdom and wealth of God upon his life.

Notice that the name of the maternal nurturer is not given in the scripture reference provided for the following sons.

Ibhar, meaning *chosen elect,* is David's eleventh son.

Elishama, meaning *whom God hears* and *God hearing*, is David's twelfth son.

Eliphelet, meaning *God his deliverance*, is David's thirteenth son.

Nogah, meaning *splendor, brightness,* and *clearness,* is David's fourteenth son.

Nepheg, meaning *weak slack sprout*, is David's fifteenth son.

Japhia, meaning *enlightening, splendid*, is David's sixteenth son.

Elishama and also called Elishua, having the same name as the twelfth son, meaning *whom God hears* and *God hearing* is David's seventeenth son.

Eliada also called Beeliada, meaning *whom God cares for*, is David's eighteenth son.

Eliphelet, having the same name as the thirteenth son, meaning *God his deliverance*, is David's nineteenth son.

~ Sons of God ~

The Lord spoke to my heart regarding the similarities of David's sons and His sons. For the scripture plainly states

"... now (presently) are we the sons of God, and it doth not yet appear what we shall be: but we know that, when he shall appear, we shall be like him; for we shall see him as he is." (1John 3:2)

Some of the similarities between David's sons and the sons of God are:

All of King David's sons are his offspring. Speaking in general terms, the various denomination of the body of Christ are all the offspring of God, the King of Kings.

All of David's sons were birthed out of an intimate relationship. The main Christian denominations account for 33% of the 98% of the world's population of religious believers (as reported by the statistics data in the Adherent.com database, which is based on self-identification). The main denominations were birthed out of a revelation from God, through His intimate relationship with a person or a group of people in pursuit of Him.

David's sons were given nurturers that carried in the womb of their spirit the key element fertilized by David's favorable attributes required to equip them to pass the greatest test of their lives. The passing of their life's greatest tests would have fortified their father's kingdom. The main denominations and their offspring were given nurturers possessing the principle elements required to accomplish the purpose that God has placed them in the earth to establish within His kingdom.

Each of David's sons possessed key elements required to exalt his kingdom. The scripture records in II Samuel 8:18 that David's sons were chief rulers of Israel; however, their united effort would have reflected a greater glory and honor upon their father's kingdom. Each portion of the body of Christ possesses key elements designed to exalt the kingdom of God. The united effort of each portion of the body of Christ reflects glory and honor unto the Lord.

~ *Groups of Christianity* ~

Each group of the body of Christ possesses various spiritual genes that are dominant within their calling. For instance, the dominant spiritual gene of the Catholic faith is structure, order, accountability, charity to the poor, and examples of consecrating ones life unto God. The Lutheran denomination, which began (16th century) while Martin Luther, a former Catholic priest, was in pursuit of God seeking a greater personal spiritual relationship, is known for reformation. The Baptist denomination is known for winning new converts on a consistent basis. The Pentecostal denomination known primarily by the fruit of The Azusa Street Revival and The Great Welsh Revival was birthed through intercession by many and later carried by William Seymour and Evan Roberts respectively. The Pentecostal denominations yet carry a strong desire and pursuit of God like Evan Roberts who prayed for 13 years for a mighty visitation of the Holy Spirit. The Pentecostal denominations also have maintained within their spiritual fiber, like William Seymour, the ability to allow the free, uninhibited flow of the power and demonstration of the Holy Ghost. This freedom and hunger for a move of God allowed Seymour to see what God had birthed through him multiplied out of Azusa Street and all across North America and into 50 nations within two years.

The combinations of the spiritual dominant genetics found in the aforementioned groups as well as countless others possess the key elements required to prepare the glorious church that God will present unto Himself. It is sad that David's sons did not combine their inherent strengths to present back unto their father a more excellent kingdom. To think that a man would have so many sons, at that time representing strength, which possessed key elements, required to produce a kingdom of great authority. However, due to a lack of discipline and unity, some of his sons caused their father's name to be shamed.

The various denominations and church groups, as the sons of God, have been given a unique opportunity to present back unto Father God a bride possessing great kingdom authority. As seen later in the life of David and his kingdom, the lack of unity among his sons did not determine his greatness or prohibit his kingdom from being the greatest ever, but his sons lost an honorable place in history as a key element reflecting his greatness. Likewise, the kingdom of God's greatness will not be inhibited by our lack of unity. His kingdom always has and always will be the greatest. I hope that we as believers will not miss this space in time to honorably reflect the greatness of God through our unity. If we would learn to appreciate the godly seed traits that abide in each group, it would be easier to embrace that which is of God within each other.

As it is with genetics, regardless of how long various species have been in existence the origins of their genetic make up can be traced. Likewise, there is not one group of Christians in which you can not find a remnant of the godly traits originally imparted by God.

For example the Catholic Church was used as a womb and incubator for church worship and practices that were later to be developed. The order and structure of most organized groups of Christianity is heavily influence by the set order and ceremonial practices established by the Catholic Church. Think about it. If you have ever attended an installation of a bishop or an overseer, the ceremonial practice typically used evolved out of the Catholic Church. Their example of order is also greatly seen in church government across the globe. Furthermore, their example of benevolence has served through the ages as God's arm of love to the orphan, widows, homeless, sick, hopeless and the unborn. The same spiritually genetic traits remain within the Catholic Church today.

It is the system of the world to judge the current state of an entity and assess its future value by its current state. The current state of the body of Christ is not as glorious as the church that Paul spoke of in his letter to the Ephesians when he compared the church to a wife.

> *"That he might present it to himself a glorious church, not having spot, or wrinkle, or any such thing; but that it should be holy and without blemish." (Ephesians 5:27)*

God's transforming power is breathing change into every portion of His body to resemble the glorious church that He will ultimately present unto Himself.

It is easy to see where man has faltered in fulfilling the will of God, as it is easy to see through church and secular history, where church groups have faltered in fulfilling the will of God.

The denomination that I have had the most affiliation with and nurturing from is about 100 years old. In those 100 years it would be fair to say that we have experienced some tremendous moments of history that have been very glorious and others which were not as glorious. I am sure that you will find this with any group that is comprised of human kind. God has allowed my primary nurturer, the Church of God in Christ to disciple, equip, train, and nurture many leaders of our day. I view the Church of God in Christ as a vital vine plant that many other organizations were able to take a piece of and plant in their own garden to bring a refreshing fervency for the things of God and a sweet exuberant fragrance of praise to the nostrils of God. I am fully persuaded that God allowed me to be nurtured by this portion of the body because they possessed the key elements that I required for the foundation of the call of God on my life.

Although I am not currently a member of the Church of God in Christ I am yet a part of them. I view this as similar to when a daughter marries, she usually adopts the name and family of her husband, but the foundation of her teaching and the rich heritage that she received from her parents is the foundation that years to come will be built on. Through the years as she takes on the wisdom of her husband's family, she is in a sense adding to her faith. Above all, she should never forget that which was pure, lovely, and of good report of her primary nurturer. If she has the seed of loyalty and wisdom, she will never mock the weaknesses of her primary nurturer to her new family, nor will she expose the weaknesses of her new family to her primary family.

If we would consider the Catholic Church has existed almost twenty times as long as, for instance, the denomination that I was nurtured through, it stands to say that they have had twenty times more years of opportunities to experience glorious and not so glorious moments. The Catholic Church as well as my spiritual nurturer, the Church of God in Christ, has key elements that serve the purpose of God. The Catholic Church, like my nurturer, has many people within its group of believers, who love and serve God with a great hunger to see the will of God fulfilled in the earth today.

I have worked with a devout, life long Catholic who issues communion to individuals in convalescent homes and to the sick and shut-in as an outreach of the Catholic Church. She expressed her concern regarding her opinion that most people view Catholics as spiritually placing Mary above Jesus. She went through great lengths to emphasize that she was taught specifically that Jesus is exalted above

Mary and any one else. She also spoke of the shame that has been placed upon them due to sins committed by some people in the priesthood. These issues are very important to her because some people outside of the Catholic faith have viewed them as a compromising group, due to the stereotype placed upon them.

I find it very interesting that any portion of the body of Christ would base their view of another group of believers on the stereotypes passed along through the years by secular media, negative reports or outside views. I am sure you are aware there are people who have left their families to serve in the priesthood and as nuns giving their lives to consecration (praying, fasting, and intercession), to serve the poor and God for twenty, thirty, forty or more years bringing glory to God. Yet, their good deeds are seldom spoken of by the secular media. However, if there is a negative report, the media will air it over and over and over again.

I hope it will suffice to say, regarding all the parts of the body of Christ, the larger the group you are associated with, the more people there are whose life and actions reflect upon your group of believers. Whether your group has 200 believers or 900 million, there are members within your group who fervently on a daily basis seek God, those who regularly seek God, those who inconsistently seek God, those who are living a carnal life, and those who have turned away from the faith but are yet affiliated, assembled, and labeled with your group. Let's not be like the world and label an entire group of believers by the few who have turned away from the faith.

The illustration of years to have not so glorious of moments can be used with almost any organized group of Christian believers. Reflecting on our local churches, denominations, and Christian groups, we are better able to see how an entire group can be labeled by the actions of past members and a relatively select few current members. With this in mind, our long-suffering with one another should increase. Our religious prejudices and stereotypes must be laid aside so that we may identify and embrace the spiritual genes of God that are in each group of believers, and connect ourselves with each group's God given gift of expertise.

Some groups possess spiritual genetics that are so identical in their spiritual expertise that one may say they are the same. An example of this can be made of David's two sons of the same name twice mentioned. Some theologians say they are the same individuals; others are of the opinion I hold that they are two separate individuals. Even though these two groups of sons carry the same name, both are essential to complete David's kingdom.

One may have asked David, which one of his sons named Elishama or Eliphelet would he want to omit, because they have the same name and carry duplicate attributes? I am sure that the father's heart of David would have conveyed although they are the same in name, their purposes are different and they each add different unique elements to his kingdom.

The body of Christ is a conglomerate of many people having various parameters of doctrinal views, religious practices, biblical interpretations and cultures that have nurtured them upon their birth into the body of Christ. There are many influences that shape the way we view and understand God. The primary influence of our perception of God is received from our primary spiritual nurturer.

As stated, our Christian nurtures are many. Some like David's children's nurturers having names more recognized than other and some are nameless. When you are birthed, schooled, or disciplined under different mothers, teachers or mentors, your way of carrying out the same given task will differ. However, the ultimate purpose of each group of the body of Christ should be to carry out the work of the Lord and accomplish His will in the earth today.

If indeed Psalm 133 was penned with David's sons in mind, these words of unity were the plea of a father to the children of his loins to dwell together in harmony. This same plea echoes the command of Father God.

The name of the religion called Christianity is a composite of many denominations and groups within each denomination. So if each denomination were viewed as a tree we would see many branches bearing fruit.

There are many, many references that list the main denominations in Christianity. The definition for Christianity is very broad. For example, the definition given from the list at religioustolerance.org is:

"…any faith group or individual that sincerely thoughtfully and devoutly regards themselves to be Christians. We consider Christian faith groups as diverse as the 1st century CE Jewish Christians, Roman Catholics, United Church members, Mormons, Unificationists, Jehovah's Witnesses and followers of hundreds of other faith groups to be Christians. We recognize that some conservative Christians have a much more restrictive definition of Christians."

The web-site also states there are 1200 Christian denominations in North America that can be divided into 15 families of denominations. The list given is as follows:

The Amish
Anglo-Israelism, British Israelism; Worldwide Church of God
The Brethren
Catholic Church (Roman Catholic)
Children of God
Christadelphians
Christian Identity Movement
Christian Science
Community of Christ/Church of Jesus Christ of Latter Day Saints

Dominion Theology
Family of Love
Gnosticism
Jehovah's Witnesses
Messianic Judaism & "Jews for Jesus"
Mormons (Church of Jesus Christ of Latter-day Saints)
The Process
Quakers (Society of Friends)
Reconstructionist Movement
Reorganized Church of Jesus Christ of Latter Day Saints: Community of Christ
Seventh-Day Adventist Church
Society of Friends (Quakers)
Theonomy
Two by Twos ("The Jesus Way", "The Church with no Name")
Unification Church
Unitarian-Universalism
United Pentecostal Church International
Unity Church in Canada
Urantia Book
Worldwide Church of God
The Way International

~ *I Am The Way* ~

While reading the various names listed as major denominations of Christianity, I was very conscious of the different methods, practices and beliefs that are represented by the list. During the search for a list that would accommodate the purpose of this book, I was very aware that by listing the major denominations given, it would present an occasion for the readers to become divided on rather or not those listed are indeed Christians. This list vividly allows us to see why the world is able to take the actions and beliefs of those listed and give a negative report reflecting on all Christians. I have questioned whether or not some of the listed groups even look upon them selves as Christians. Please be mindful that religioustolerance.org is not necessarily a Christian organization; therefore, their view of Christian groups may differ greatly from yours.

I decided not to take the easy way out by only listing the three less controversial Christian groups: Roman Catholicism, Eastern Orthodoxy and Protestantism. I sincerely hope that in light of the effort given, we will view the given list with the discerning factor that Jesus spoke of:

> *John 10:1 Verily, verily, I say unto you, He that entereth not by the door into the sheepfold, but climbeth up some other way, the same is a thief and a robber.*
>
> *2 But he that entereth in by the door is the shepherd of the sheep.*
>
> *3 To him the porter openeth; and the sheep hear his voice: and he calleth his own sheep by name, and leadeth them out.*
>
> *4 And when he putteth forth his own sheep, he goeth before them, and the sheep follow him: for they know his voice.*
>
> *5 And a stranger will they not follow, but will flee from him: for they know not the voice of strangers.*
>
> *6 This parable spake Jesus unto them: but they understood not what things they were which he spake unto them.*
>
> *7 Then said Jesus unto them again, Verily, verily, I say unto you, I am the door of the sheep.*
>
> *8 All that ever came before me are thieves and robbers: but the sheep did not hear them.*

> 9 I am the door: by me if any man enter in, he shall be saved, and shall go in and out, and find pasture.
> 10 The thief cometh not, but for to steal, and to kill, and to destroy: I am come that they might have life, and that they might have it more abundantly.
> 11 I am the good shepherd: the good shepherd giveth his life for the sheep.
> 12 But he that is an hireling, and not the shepherd, whose own the sheep are not, seeth the wolf coming, and leaveth the sheep, and fleeth: and the wolf catcheth them, and scattereth the sheep.
> 13 The hireling fleeth, because he is an hireling, and careth not for the sheep.
> 14 I am the good shepherd, and know my sheep, and am known of mine.
> 15 As the Father knoweth me, even so know I the Father: and I lay down my life for the sheep.
> 16 And other sheep I have, which are not of this fold: them also I must bring, and they shall hear my voice; and there shall be one fold, and one shepherd.

It is through the preceding scriptures that Jesus reminds us we are of the sheep of His pasture if we have entered through Him (His shed blood for the remission of our sins). Any other way of entering into the family of God is illegal (i.e. v. 8 thieves and robbers).

It is through the shed blood of Jesus that we each possess the spiritual genetics of God. If we are able to glean the spiritual genetics which are true, virtuous and of good report from each other, we will be a part of the church that Christ presents unto Himself as a glorious church not having spot, wrinkle, blemish or any such thing, and holy without blemish.

~ Subduing Division ~

Throughout North American history, at times of crisis or while standing on the threshold of change, there were voices of key individuals stating that we must unify ourselves and become as one to conquer our present and potential enemies. The crowds answered with a resounding "Yes". However, when key individuals addressed the racial social opposing factors of unity stating, if we are to achieve the level of unity that conquers our enemies we must look people who we have shunned, in their faces and identify them as Americans having the same value, rights, and privileges as others, the actions of the crowd spoke of a people not willing to pay the price of unity.

The apostle Paul also questioned division among the Corinthians saying:

> ***I Corinthians 1:10*** *Now I beseech you, brethren, by the name of our Lord Jesus Christ, that ye all speak the same thing, and that there be no divisions among you; but that ye be perfectly joined together in the same mind and in the same judgment.* ***11*** *For it hath been declared unto me of you, my brethren, by them which are of the house of Chloe, that there are contentions among you.* ***12*** *Now this I say, that every one of you saith, I am of Paul; and I of Apollos; and I of Cephas; and I of Christ.* ***13*** **<u>*Is Christ divided?*</u>** *was Paul crucified for you? or were ye baptized in the name of Paul?*

Today, in the church world, if we are ever to really subdue the divisions among denominations and Christian organizations, we must look brothers and sisters of other portions of the body in their spiritual and natural eyes, recognizing and validating their role and significance in the body of Christ.

I have observed this same type of division while observing the behavior of children who have the same father but different mothers. I noticed that there is usually an inherent desire to prove to the other siblings they have shared a special time with their father, or know something their father only told them, or possess something their father only gave them in an attempt to have their other siblings perceive them as the favored one. I also noticed that regardless how often the father attempts to instill love among his children, if their individual nurturers (mothers) do not cultivate the father's bond of love among the children, it usually does not take deep root. The children usually label themselves by their nurturer and identify and segregate themselves from their other siblings rather than identifying themselves as one because of their father's blood flowing through their veins. Furthermore, it is not uncommon for children having the same father but a different nurturer to question later in life whether or not a sibling is of *their* father's seed.

The same can be said about the Christian community. We all like David's sons, have the same Father but different nurturers. Due to the fact that we have various nurturers, there has been the desire to prove some have experienced a more intimate time with the Father, or know something the Father only told them, thereby possessing something the Father only gave them.

I am quite aware some denominations and groups are more pliable and open to spiritual realms and possess a balance that others may not have yet tapped into, but that does not make those having deeper levels of experience more valuable to the FATHER. He may entrust them with more, but to assume an extraordinary level of spirituality causes the Father to select one as a favorite would be similar to believing a father having an infant and a teenager would favor the mature one above the infant. Whether a church group has the spiritual maturity level equivalent to a kindergartner student or a Harvard University graduate, the love of the Father, at each level, is the same. God is also requiring that our love for one another mirror His love.

David had many sons but surely his love for them was based on the fact they were of his seed. Through the new birth we have the seed of God. We are the sons of God and His love for us, as groups of Christians, spans each level of maturity in the same way.

I look for the day that the body of Christ will seek to excel in loving one another. Wouldn't it be amazing if all over the globe, groups of leaders from various portions of the body of Christ came together laying their greatest needs (spiritual development, organizational skills, community outreach, leadership skills, financial development, spiritual gifts, financial investment, developing and maintaining multicultural congregations, structuring help ministries, youth programs, church employees, how to recover from scandals) on the table and their main objective was to find a way to strengthen and equip each other, without any strings attached, in confidentiality, and in an effort to show the love of Christ? This may sound foreign and impossible, but so was the thought of the Berlin Wall falling before 1996.

It is this type of love that will cause us to win our world. This is the hour God is saying again:

John 13: 34; A new commandment I give unto you, That ye love one another; as I have loved you, that ye also love one another.
35 By this shall all men know that ye are my disciples, if ye have love one to another.

Walking in His love is the truest test of discipleship and becoming a matured body. Paul said it like this:

> *1 Corinthians 13:1 Though I speak with the tongues of men and of angels and have not charity I am become as sounding brass, or a tinkling cymbal.*
> *2 And though I have the gift of prophecy, and understand all mysteries, and all knowledge; and though I have all faith, so that I could remove mountains, and have not charity I am nothing.*

Have you ever seen a portion of the body of Christ that take pride in knowing God in a more intimate way because they excel in loving their neighbor? I'm sure that there are some that are excelling in love but because of their maturity level they only boast in Him. However, I have heard Christians boast of their financial blessings, gifts of faith, depth of the Word of God, gifts of the Spirit, spiritual visitations, liberality, holy living and modest dress.

We are all the Father's children and He desires that we would recognize and value each other in our specific callings. As it was with David's sons, God has given every portion of the body of Christ nurturers to develop specific areas of expertise. Thereby, His body is equipped with every key tool required to strengthen His kingdom in the earth, win our world and present unto Him a glorious church.

~ The Call to Unite ~

As I am writing, I am reminded of John the Baptist, who came preaching, *"...Prepare ye the way of the Lord"*. John's salutation did not make Jesus the Christ come on the scene. Jesus was already on His way to fulfill His purpose in obedience to the timing of God the Father. However, John, in obedience, spoke out prophetically to the hearts of men. I am saying, through the pages of this book, that God is going to bring true unity to the body of Christ that will answer the earnest expectation of the world.

Romans 8:19 For the earnest expectation of the creature waiteth for the manifestation of the sons of God.

Unity does not begin at a gathering of reconciliation. Unity begins when we decide that we will do as Noah's sons who walked backward and covered their father's nakedness. Unity begins when we decide that we will not tell about an unfavorable incident concerning a person in the body of Christ. Unity begins when we stop speaking negative against the church down the street. Unity begins when we make a decision that we are in prayerful support for the entire body of Christ. Not with respect of group, denomination, race, nationality, or social status. Unity begins when we pray that the glory of the Lord God Jehovah will cover the earth as the waters cover the sea. Having a prayerful plea that the abundance of God, the presence of God, the manifestation of the power of God would be experienced in a realm not known to the earth before.

I perceive the people of the Lord are at a ripened stage to reap the greatest spiritual harvest the world has ever known. I am also fully persuaded that our greatest challenge will not be false religions, malicious press attacks, and lack of provisions or political persuasions. We are now in the set hour, just as it was with Elijah (I Kings 18:19), our God will show Himself to be the God above all other gods. We will not be defeated by false, or in some cases even true malicious reports because the sword of the Lord shall go out against them who purposely come against the people of the Lord to defame God, and people will say in the aftermath of the sword of God, "Wasn't that the reporter who sought to bring down the servant of the Lord?" This will happen to the point that many unbelievers will fear the Lord. Furthermore, money will not be a hindrance to the greatest harvest. Ministries and servants that God has entrusted with one, five and even ten talents in the past, showing themselves to be good stewards walking in reverential integrity, shall be given supernatural provision for the vision of the Lord. Neither will political policies be a deterrent to the plans of God. He will raise unsuspecting individuals to political assignments to accomplish His will. I dare to say that division is our greatest enemy, and supernatural UNITY shall be the sword of the Lord that shall cut off the head of this foe. Our unity shall be even as the rock from David's sling that served as the blow which brought Goliath down, rendering him powerless against God's people. The spirit of God shall take the enemy's sword of division, devised for our demise, and turn it on him, cutting off the head of our enemy and we shall see him no more.

~~~~~~~~~~~~~~~~ Selah ~~~~~~~~~~~~~~~~

Chapter IV

Moses

Psalms 133:1 Behold, how good and how pleasant it is for brethren to dwell together in unity!
> **2 It is like the precious ointment upon the head, that ran down upon the beard, even Aaron's beard: that went down to the skirts of his garments;**
> *3 As the dew of Hermon, and as the dew that descended upon the mountains of Zion: for there the LORD commanded the blessing, even life for evermore.*

One of the most memorable leaders of all times is Moses. He was born with a death sentence upon his head, but lived through the divine protection and intervention of God. Imagine what this great Hebrew-Egyptian-Meridian taught leader would have accomplished if he had been surrounded by a group of people who were united to rehearse in his hearing the word of the Lord spoken to him.

> *Exodus 3:6 Moreover He said, I am the God of thy father, the God of Abraham, the God of Isaac, and*

> the God of Jacob. And Moses hid his face; for he was afraid to look upon God.
>
> 7 And the LORD said, I have surely seen the affliction of my people which are in Egypt, and have heard their cry by reason of their taskmasters; for I know their sorrows;
>
> 8 And I am come down to deliver them out of the hand of the Egyptians, and to bring them up out of that land unto a good land and a large, unto a land flowing with milk and honey; unto the place of the Canaanites, and the Hittites, and the Amorites, and the Perizzites, and the Hivites, and the Jebusites.
>
> 9 Now therefore, behold, the cry of the children of Israel is come unto me: and I have also seen the oppression wherewith the Egyptians oppress them.
>
> 10 Come now therefore, and I will send thee unto Pharaoh, that thou mayest bring forth my people the children of Israel out of Egypt.

We will never know the extended role Moses would have played if the children of Israel had been working together, skillfully playing their roles in the fulfillment of the purpose of God for his life, which was to escort them into their covenant promised land. I think it would not be too presumptuous to say that this courageous leader would have led them through the eleven days journey, which they traveled for 40 years, in less than eleven days. If the children of Israel had entered the Promise Land eleven days after the exodus of Egypt, Moses would have had 39 years and 354 days or more to complete another assignment for the Lord.

When you have a submitted non-murmuring group of believers working towards a specified, God ordained destination, they enter into a realm that is not confined to our physical ability or earthly time frames. Groups of people operating at this level of unity are candidates to "pick up their skirts as the prophet of old and out run the chariot."

Many times God will allow supernatural church growth, increase in finances, or in this scenario, He could have permitted travel without the restraints of time to make an example or speak prophetically to a group of people. God could have allowed them to make the journey in seven days to signify He was causing them after four hundred years of captivity to enter into a place of rest. God could very easily have allowed the journey to be accomplished in eight days, signifying a day of new beginnings for the children of Israel in the land of promise. However, the children of Israel were not in unity with the vision of God so they experienced forty years of desert travel.

~ Desert Travel ~

It was not Moses' lot to lead a group of people cheering, "Go ahead man of God, we are upholding you in words, deeds, and prayers." No, Moses was not assigned to that group of people. He was given the assignment to lead a people who, through their oppression and bondage, had taken on the habits of mumbling, grumbling, complaining and despising their leader. The level of poisonous murmuring, complaining and strife which the children of Israel perfected, was so lethal that with the exception of Joshua and Caleb, the entire adult population of those brought out of Egypt was consumed. Now that is a plague!

This speaks volumes to me concerning the doors of every evil work that strife opens. Strife, along with other negative behavior patterns, includes mumbling and complaining. Strife is solely listed in the Bible as the key that opens the door to E-V-E-R-Y evil work. Every evil work includes, but is not restricted to lawlessness, disobedience, consumption of ones life without productivity, lack of direction, and being deceived by the enemy.

Moses, after withstanding the resistance of Pharaoh to let the people of the Lord go out of Egypt, had to endure the resistance of the children of Israel. I would liken their resistance to a lifeguard attempting to rescue an individual from imminent death.

The scene goes something like this: We have a person who does not have the ability to swim in deep waters; however, because he has entered the water during high tide, he is swiftly swept into the deepest parts of the ocean. He is entirely at the mercy of the brutal engulfing waves tossing his body hopelessly as he cries out for a deliverer. At last, before he is submerged for the third time into the deep, his cry is heard in the distance, and a lifeguard is sent out with the commission to rescue him.

Every element of the deliverer's life was strategically choreographed for this hour of deliverance. His very name means draw out or drawn out of water. His training was exclusively and extensively designed to deliver those who become endangered while swimming, playing, surfing or carrying out other water activities.

This potential drowning victim is overwhelmingly grateful that someone has heard his cry and has come to rescue him. However, after seeing and mentally assessing the person as one who is a sent to deliver him from the captivating waters, the victim continues, as if by habitual reflex, flinging himself about, overcome with doubt and fear. The lifeguard continually repeats, "Relax. I've got you. Don't fight me. Rest in my arms. Just be still! I will take you to safety. Everything is all right. I am sent to deliver you."

But NO! This person is not listening (comprehending and following directions). His actions speak loudly that he does not trust the deliverer. He continues his habitual survival tactics, fighting the water and the deliverer. After a period of this continued behavior the deliverer becomes frustrated jeopardizing his own life by not utilizing the crucial instructions he received during the time of extensive training. In one split second, he reverts to a character flaw that has haunted him throughout his entire training. The numerous other times that he was in a similar situation and became angry it was not fatal, yet because of the depth of water and *timing* of this incident, this type of character flaw is now lethal.

In Moses' case, the lethal character flaw was anger. After the children of Israel had murmured against Moses and Aaron again because there was no water, God gave them specific instructions to provide water for the Israelites.

> *(Numbers 20:8-12) 8 Take the rod, and gather thou the assembly together, thou, and Aaron thy brother, and speak ye unto the rock before their eyes; and it shall give forth his water, and thou shalt bring forth to them water out of the rock: so thou shalt give the congregation and their beasts drink.*
>
> *9 And Moses took the rod from before the LORD, as he commanded him.*
>
> *10 And Moses and Aaron gathered the congregation together before the rock, and he said unto them, Hear now, ye rebels; must we fetch you water out of this rock?*
>
> *11 And Moses lifted up his hand, and with his rod he smote the rock twice: and the water came out abundantly, and the congregation drank, and their beasts also.*
>
> *12 And the LORD spake unto Moses and Aaron, Because ye believed me not, to sanctify me in the eyes of the children of Israel, therefore ye shall not bring this congregation into the land which I have given them.*

This is a familiar passage of scripture were we plainly see God's command that Moses would speak to the rock before their eyes and it shall give forth water. Moses had dealt with their endless murmuring for 40 years. The first group has died off and now the remaining group is carrying out the inherited, learned habitual behavior of complaining. Moses disobeyed God during his angry reply to their constant murmuring saying must <u>we</u> fetch you water out of this rock, and smote the rock twice.

In the eyes of the disgruntled congregation, the purpose is served. They now have water to appease their fleshly desire. But in the spirit realm, they have lost their spiritual father due to their endless murmuring and cries of the flesh. Thereafter, Moses and Aaron were told that they would not accompany the Israelites into the land of promise.

~ *Promise Land Hindrances* ~

How many of our spiritual leaders have we vexed crying for fleshly gratification, to the point that in their anger or desire to please, they produced something out of the flesh that should only have been produced by the Spirit? Is it okay to say that this type of behavior has caused their spiritual destiny to not be fulfilled because they did not produce it through the Spirit?

One may say this is such a menial offense. Yet, as you have grown in the things of God, I am sure you have become painfully aware that what God allowed in your primary development is not allowed after entering certain levels of relationship with Him.

There is usually one thing that keeps coming to surface when God speaks to our heart, which has been planted like a weed, by the enemy to serve as a potential eliminator to our possession of the Promised Land.

Unity

We all know within our hearts the one issue that God ever so gently begins to tug at, saying:

(At level 1) Lay _____ (fill in the blank) aside.

(Level 2) Separate your self from _____.

(Level 3) Your next level depends upon your discipline in the area of _____.

(Level 4) If you choose not to deal with _____ the day usually arrives that you see the promise land and denied access, or see someone else doing what He initially assigned to you with the full knowledge that you have been eliminated, because of _____.

It is when this occurs that regardless how many accomplishments people lay to your credit and God's glory; you yet possess an empty place that could only be filled by *completing* His assignment for your life.

There are many views as to why this one final act eliminated Moses from entering the Promise Land. One of the reasons most often given is that the rock represents the Messiah, and when Moses struck the rock twice, it was symbolic of crucifying Jesus twice. Therefore, Moses was eliminated from entering into the promise of God because he did not obey God and sanctify the Lord before the people. Likewise, Aaron was restricted from entering the Promise Land because he did not stop or correct Moses. Aaron would have been well within his rights, to correct Moses, because God gave the instructions to both of them.

One could easily argue that Moses was beside himself after years of desert travel, coping with grief associated with the death of his sister and being greatly provoked by the children of Israel's constant murmuring. There is nothing like mumbling, grumbling and complaining that grates against the enthusiasm of leadership. The children of Israel had perfected the technique of synchronized complaining to an art form. Think about it, after seeing the miraculous hand of God work mightily on their behalf and in Moses' favor, the

Children of Israel yet mumbled, grumbled and complained. Time and time again the Israelites charged Moses unfairly:

1. Accused Moses of bringing them out into the wilderness to die. (Exodus 14:11, 12).
2. Children of Israel murmured because the water was bitter. This occurs within days after the Red Sea was divided and used as a weapon to destroy their enemy (Exodus 15: 22-25).
3. Murmured because they were hungry (Exodus 16:2, 3). During this tantrum, Moses prompts us to see that when we murmur against who God has placed in leadership we are actually murmuring against God (Exodus 16:8).
4. Argued with Moses because of thirst (Ex 17:2-4).
5. Aaron and the people complained and built a golden calf because Moses was gone hearing from God for a period of time that they thought was too long.

I have many times heard people quote the scripture saying, "What shall we say to these things. If God be for us who can be against us?" During my youth, my father served as a pastor. It was during that time that I first experienced the unconditional sacrifices that are a daily part of a leader and their family's life. I was also able to see how people may cry, "Blessed is he who comes in the name of the Lord" this week, and "crucify him" next week. Whenever I heard the aforementioned passage of scripture read, I would silently answer the preacher saying, *"The people can be against you."* Nevertheless, after "living on" as my mother would say, I have come to the conclusion that if God is for us, there is nothing that can stand against us.

There is another reason that is seen through the lives of their ancestors that I view as an element of understanding why Moses was not allowed to enter into the land of promise.

In the 34th chapter of Genesis, there is given the first account of rape. The prince of the Hivites, Shechem, defiled Dinah, Jacob and Leah's daughter. Shechem's father Hamor inquired of an honorable way to ensure Dinah's hand in marriage to his son. Thereafter, the sons of Jacob used religious beliefs to clothe their deceptive motives for revenge.

The brothers of Dinah agreed that if the Hivites would be circumcised they would allow their sister, who was being held in Shechem's house, to marry the prince. The writer notes that the heart of the prince was better than all of the other Hivites. Considering his actions of rape, I am not impressed and neither were her brothers.

The Hivites may have viewed Jacob's son's demand of circumcision as a strategic political way, in their favor, to gain an alliance as well as a way to alleviate the anger of the Israelites.

Three days after the circumcision of the Hivites, the most painful time of the healing process, Simeon and Levi in their *anger*, killed Shechem, Hamor, and all of the Hivites' men of valor. This greatly displeased Jacob and in his dying moments, he reflects upon their sin, pronouncing the judgment of the curse upon their ANGER.

> *(Genesis 49:5) Simeon and Levi are brethren; instruments of cruelty are in their habitations.*
> *(Genesis 49:7 "Cursed be their anger, for it was fierce; and their wrath, for it was cruel; I will divide them in Jacob, and scatter them in Israel."*

It is especially interesting Jacob said he would divide them in Jacob and scatter them in Israel. Jacob means supplanter and trickery, and Israel is the name associated with the promise of God given after Jacob was changed. So he divided Simeon and Levi in their trickery (Jacob). Upon possession of the Promised Land the tribe of Levi is scattered as priest in the land of promise (Israel), throughout the appointed land of the various tribes of Israel.

It is to be noted that the tribe of Levi being scattered throughout Canaan was a reflection upon Jacob's curse of their anger and yet God's blessed selection of them as priests unto Him.

Is it possible that Moses and Aaron, being of the tribe of Levi – displayed the seed of anger again that was seen in Levi and Simeon and God said once again I will divide them in their anger? Could it be that until the children of Israel possessed the land of promise that the consequences (the curse upon their anger), to divide them in Jacob, was in effect? We know man's anger never produces the sanctification or the setting apart for the glory of God, his marvelous handiwork: such as water coming from a rock by the spoken command. So they were not allowed to enter in because they did not display the character that sanctifies God before His people.

I would imagine that the most devastating moment in the life of Moses was not when he was weaned and severed from the loving arms of his birth mother for the purposes of God, nor when he discovered that someone knew he had, in anger, killed the Egyptian. It was not even when, in man's eyes, he had been reduced from living as a prince to a lowly shepherd. His greatest moment of devastation was not when God told him that he must go back to Pharaoh's house with a message, telling him the slaves which he laid unbearable burdens upon, did not belong to him but unto HIM; furthermore, the appointed time had come that he must release them from serving him so that they could serve HIM. The most devastating hour was not when he faced the threat of being stoned by the Children of Israel because they had come to a place of bitter waters three days after seeing one of the greatest historical miracles at the Red Sea. I assure you, that all of these incidents pale greatly in the light of the soul wrenching devastation experienced, when upon Mount Carmel, he looked over into the land of promise, knowing that he was eliminated as the leader to escort Gods people into the Promise Land.

Imagine hearing the voice that had become the audible coolant of comfort through the forty years of desert travel saying, *"Go to Mount Carmel and die."* What an incredible moment of devastation!

It is often after a person has seen they will not reach their deepest desire and goal that you see the real heart of the individual towards the people. After Moses received the sentence pronounced by God upon Aaron and himself, he did not say, "Well you rebels are on your own from here on. I have given my life for you people and your murmuring and complaining has, at last, cost me the victorious summation of my life. I should have agreed with God the numerous times that He wanted to destroy you people. Figure out for yourselves how to enter into the Promise Land." No! It is not recorded that Moses uttered such words. Moses possessed the true heart of a leader and shepherd.

Immediately after hearing he would die without entering the Promise Land, Moses makes an attempt to acquire permission of passage for the children of Israel through Edom. This was a very sensitive matter because Seir was the land where the descendants of Esau, also called Edom, lived. Esau's descendants had not forgotten how Jacob (Israel) had tricked their forefather out of his inheritance. Furthermore, the children of Israel could not fight against them because the Lord had commanded them not to uproot the descendants of Esau, because God would not give them Mount Seir, the land He had given Esau and his descendants as a possession.

Family matters are always a sticky situation. A zealous novice would not have possessed the knowledge required to follow the final tracking steps of God into the Promise Land. Only a person who has acquired the knowledge of God through the process of communing with Him on the back side of the desert, hearing His voice out of a burning bush, choosing to turn aside to see the initial great wonder of God, seeing Him turn water into blood, thickening the darkness before the eyes of His enemies, cutting off the first born of the those who opposed his command, seeing God roll back the Red Sea with an east wind and lay dry ground before you so you will not fall before your enemies and then subduing your enemies with the same water, being a person who twice spent 40 days receiving instruction from the mouth of God; only a person who has withstood the trying and discipline of God would have the innate spiritual ability required to deal with the past family wound of Jacob and Esau.

Moses is faithful to the end, leading the people of the Lord around this encounter through Kadesh, the desert of Paran. Kadesh is where the original account of a land flowing with milk and honey was given to the Israelites. Isn't that just like God to bring them back to the place where He first unveiled His purposed inheritance for Israel, right before releasing them into their destiny? What a picture of a people coming full circle!

Kadesh is also the place where Korah, a Levite, along with descendants of Reuben, the sons of Eliab, and a leader named On together with 250 of the princes (men of renown) of Israel came against Moses. There they challenged Moses authority declaring the whole congregation was holy, and that Moses and Aaron had elevated themselves unto the Lord.

There may be a few of you leaders who have heard the words, "You are a man just like me and I hear from God too." This is the same type of declaration Korah and his followers made to Moses.

Moses, in an effort to dissuade them, reminds them God had chosen Korah and the others as Levites to do the service of the tabernacle (i.e. preparing sacrifices for the service of the Lord) and to minister before the people. This was not enough for Korah. He thought he should perform the assignment given to Aaron. Korah's seed of discord produced an earthquake and fire that consumed him, his family and all that pertained to him and the families of the other main instigators of discord. Over a thousand years later, the writer penned the word *"Woe unto them who sow discord."* The same God that abhorred discord then is the same today and He changes not.

As you see, Moses is very familiar with Kadesh. This is the place of decision, visitation, and burial of his sister Miriam. Moses, the true shepherd, led God's people through the peaceful trail way onward toward the Promised Land and released them with his blessing.

~ *Preparing the Priest and Tabernacle* ~

Despite the fact that Moses did not enter into the Promise Land, the face to face encounters which he experienced with God served as literal instructions to those under the law and as a type and shadow giving the church today key insight into approaching Father God.

> *"Who serve unto the example and shadow of heavenly things, as Moses was admonished of God when he was about to make the tabernacle: for, See, saith he, that thou make all things according to the pattern shewed to thee in the mount." (Hebrews 8:5)*

The passage is in reference to the instructions received during the forty days, which Moses experienced with God on Mt. Sinai. Through the ageless word of God we are able to experience the time of visitation. It is more than history, and greater than a story. It is a visitation, which transcends time. Through the light of His word we are able to capture

His voice now as though we were there then. Hear the word of the Lord:

> *Exodus 25:1 And the Lord spake unto Moses, saying,*
> *2 Speak unto the children of Israel, that they bring me an offering: of every man that giveth it willingly with his heart ye shall take my offering.*
> *3 And this is the offering which ye shall take of them; gold, and silver, and brass,*
> *4 And blue, and purple, and scarlet, and fine linen, and goats' hair,*
> *5 And rams' skins dyed red, and badgers' skins, and shittim wood,*
> *6 Oil for the light, spices for anointing oil, and for sweet incense,*
> *7 Onyx stones, and stones to be set in the ephod, and in the breastplate.*
> *8 And let them make me a sanctuary; that I may dwell among them.*
> *9 According to all that I shew thee, after the pattern of the tabernacle, and the pattern of all the instruments thereof, even so shall ye make it.*

God continues speaking with Moses concerning the pattern and measurements of the tabernacle and the furniture to be placed therein. Immediately after completing the instruction of the tabernacle, God continues with the instructions for the holy garments that His selected high priest would wear to minister unto Him in the priest's office. Through this scripture, one may see the offering to the Lord was not only to provide for the needs of the tabernacle but also the needs of the minister.

Exodus 28:1 And take thou unto thee Aaron thy brother, and his sons with him, from among the children of Israel, that he may minister unto me in the priest's office, even Aaron, Nadab and Abihu, Eleazar and Ithamar, Aaron's sons.

2 *And thou shalt make holy garments for Aaron thy brother for glory and for beauty.*

3 *And thou shalt speak unto all that are wise hearted, whom I have filled with the spirit of wisdom, that they may make Aaron's garments to consecrate him, that he may minister unto me in the priest's office.*

4 *And these are the garments which they shall make; a breastplate, and an ephod, and a robe, and a broidered coat, a mitre, and a girdle: and they shall make holy garments for Aaron thy brother, and his sons, that he may minister unto me in the priest's office.*

5 *And they shall take gold, and blue, and purple, and scarlet, and fine linen.*

6 *And they shall make the ephod of gold, of blue, and of purple, of scarlet, and fine twined linen, with cunning work.*

7 *It shall have the two shoulderpieces thereof joined at the two edges thereof; and so it shall be joined together.*

8 *And the curious girdle of the ephod, which is upon it, shall be of the same, according to the work thereof; even of gold, of blue, and purple, and scarlet, and fine twined linen.*

9 *And thou shalt take two onyx stones, and grave on them the names of the children of Israel:*

10 *Six of their names on one stone, and the other six names of the rest on the other stone, according to their birth.*

11 With the work of an engraver in stone, like the engravings of a signet, shalt thou engrave the two stones with the names of the children of Israel: thou shalt make them to be set in ouches of gold.

12 And thou shalt put the two stones upon the shoulders of the ephod for stones of memorial unto the children of Israel: and Aaron shall bear their names before the Lord upon his two shoulders for a memorial.

13 And thou shalt make ouches of gold;

14 And two chains of pure gold at the ends; of wreathen work shalt thou make them, and fasten the wreathen chains to the ouches.

15 And thou shalt make the breastplate of judgment with cunning work; after the work of the ephod thou shalt make it; of gold, of blue, and of purple, and of scarlet, and of fine twined linen, shalt thou make it.

16 Foursquare it shall be being doubled; a span shall be the length thereof, and a span shall be the breadth thereof.

17 And thou shalt set in it settings of stones, even four rows of stones: the first row shall be a sardius, a topaz, and a carbuncle: this shall be the first row.

18 And the second row shall be an emerald, a sapphire, and a diamond.

19 And the third row a ligure, an agate, and an amethyst.

20 And the fourth row a beryl, and an onyx, and a jasper: they shall be set in gold in their inclosings.

21 And the stones shall be with the names of the children of Israel, twelve, according to their names, like the engravings of a signet; every one with his name shall they be according to the twelve tribes.

God continues His instructions in verse 29.

29 And Aaron shall bear the names of the children of Israel in the breastplate of judgment upon his heart, when he goeth in unto the holy place, for a memorial before the Lord continually.
31 And thou shalt make the robe of the ephod all of blue.
32 And there shall be an hole in the top of it, in the midst thereof: it shall have a binding of woven work round about the hole of it, as it were the hole of an habergeon, that it be not rent.
33 And beneath upon the hem of it thou shalt make pomegranates of blue, and of purple, and of scarlet, round about the hem thereof; and bells of gold between them round about:
34 A golden bell and a pomegranate, a golden bell and a pomegranate, upon the hem of the robe round about.
35 And it shall be upon Aaron to minister: and his sound shall be heard when he goeth in unto the holy place before the Lord, and when he cometh out, that he die not.
36 And thou shalt make a plate of pure gold, and grave upon it, like the engravings of a signet, HOLINESS TO THE LORD.
37 And thou shalt put it on a blue lace, that it may be upon the mitre; upon the forefront of the mitre it shall be.
38 And it shall be upon Aaron's forehead, that Aaron may bear the iniquity of the holy things, which the children of Israel shall hallow in all their holy

gifts; and it shall be always upon his forehead, that they may be accepted before the Lord.

39 And thou shalt embroider the coat of fine linen, and thou shalt make the mitre of fine linen, and thou shalt make the girdle of needlework.

40 And for Aaron's sons thou shalt make coats, and thou shalt make for them girdles, and bonnets shalt thou make for them, for glory and for beauty.

41 And thou shalt put them upon Aaron thy brother, and his sons with him; and shalt anoint them, and consecrate them, and sanctify them, that they may minister unto me in the priest's office.

43 And they shall be upon Aaron, and upon his sons, when they come in unto the tabernacle of the congregation, or when they come near unto the altar to minister in the holy place; that they bear not iniquity, and die: it shall be a statute for ever unto him and his seed after him.

Exodus 29:1 And this is the thing that thou shalt do unto them to hallow them, to minister unto me in the priest's office: Take one young bullock, and two rams without blemish,

2 And unleavened bread, and cakes unleavened tempered with oil, and wafers unleavened anointed with oil: of wheaten flour shalt thou make them.

3 And thou shalt put them into one basket, and bring them in the basket, with the bullock and the two rams.

4 And Aaron and his sons thou shalt bring unto the door of the tabernacle of the congregation, and shalt wash them with water.

5 And thou shalt take the garments, and put upon Aaron the coat, and the robe of the ephod, and the ephod, and the breastplate, and gird him with the curious girdle of the ephod:
6 And thou shalt put the mitre upon his head, and put the holy crown upon the mitre.

The scriptures allow us to see a foreshadow of the combined work of the people preparing the priest (ultimately Jesus at the right hand of the Father) to minister before the Lord and make intercession on their behalf.

In Exodus 25:2 God extended an invitation unto those who were willing to give; an opportunity to give the supplies required in making the tabernacle and the priestly garments. This invitation included yielding their talents, skills and substance.

For instance, the gold, symbolizing divinity, and silver, symbolic of redemption, required refining, which takes the skills of a refiner. To produce the four kinds of linen not only required skill to weave and spin, but also required the material needed to produce the specified colors. To have the material required for producing the color blue, symbolizing the Son of God, for the linen, one must retrieve cerulean mussel shells. The color purple, symbolizing royalty, was made from murex snail's secretions. The color scarlet, symbolizing the Savior, was made from the glowworm. To give an offering of goat hair, symbolizing sin, and rams skin, symbolizing substitution offering and consecration, required various other skills and tools, as well as the handwork of those who herd such animals. The offering of badger skin could only be acquired by catching a badger, an aquatic mammal (related to the manatee and modern day dolphins), and skinning it. This offering required many skills as well. The offering of shittim, symbolizing flesh, comes from the acacia tree. This very durable wood is found in the Sinai Peninsula and

Egypt. This offering too, was one that had to be gathered, and required great work to produce a finished product. To produce the olive oil, symbolic of the Holy Spirit, used to maintain the flame of the candlestick involved the collection of the olive and the crushing process that produced the olive oil. The demand of skills such as carving wood, creating works of metal, brass and silver to complete the furnishings and making of the tabernacle was a combined effort as well. All of the combined efforts and offerings provided a place of habitation, where God met with man.

This is the order of the tabernacle. The priest would enter the gate, which gave entrance to the court. Entering the court the priest first came to the brazen altar of sacrifice. There is an open courtyard between the brazen altar and the brazen laver. The brazen laver, which was used by the priest to wash his hands and feet before entering the holy place to minister unto the Lord, is located east to the entrance of the Holy Place. Facing west inside of the Holy Place, to the right is the table of shewbread. On the left is the golden candlestick. Beyond the table of shewbread and the golden candlestick, centered in front of the veil, is the golden altar of incense. The veil of entrance to the Most Holy Place is directly behind the golden altar of incense. It is beyond the veil that the priest experienced the very presence of God.

Some may say we have experienced the beyond the veil visitation. I assure you that positionally, in Christ, we have experienced beyond the veil as a visitation. Key word is v-i-s-i-t-a-t-i-o-n. I challenge you not to assume, that just because we have the precious redemption wrought through the death of Jesus Christ, which gives us direct access to the Father, that we have experienced the full measure of His presence beyond the veil.

One may say if they experience Him on that level in the Old Testament most surely as New Testament believers we have gone beyond that experience. I would like to pose a few questions for thought. Do we, on a continual basis, talk face to face with God, like Moses? Do you own tablets having commandments written with His penmanship? Has the earth swallowed up your enemies? Do you experience the glory of God in a dimension that would kill you if you choose not to walk at a level that is conducive to His manifested miraculous presence? Trust me; there is a level of fellowship with Him that most people have not even begun to tap into. We, as the church and grace age, have access to a dimension of glory that was not available to the Israelites. This level of fellowship can only be experienced as we abide in a supernatural level of unity with God and each other. It is at that level that we will have the abiding, beyond the veil, presence.

It is to be noted that the scripture reading allows us to see where some of the same material used for the tabernacle was also used for the priest's garments or offerings.

The cunning work and details necessary in preparing, according to instruction, both the tabernacle and the priest's garments required an enormous group effort.

Exodus 31:2 gives record of the call of God upon Bezaleel, the son of Uri, of the tribe of Judah. God chose Bezaleel specifically as an artisan. He was given the task to create and oversee the making of the shapes of the jewels, carve the wood, the tabernacle of meetings, the ark of the Testimony, the mercy seat, furniture of the tabernacle, the lamp stand, the utensils, the laver, the garments of ministry, the holy garments for Aaron and his sons, the anointing oil, and sweet incense for the holy place. According to the New Open Bible the definition of Bezaleel's name is in the shadow or protection of God. God chose someone who was living in His shadow to create a place of dwelling for Him. What a life! What a call!

~ *Clothing the Priest* ~

There are many revelations of Christ and His body within the carried out order of the structure of the temple, the furnishings, the priest, and the priestly garments and vesture. I would like to focus on the combined effort of the priestly garment and vesture in light of God's people unifying their skills, giftings and talents to produce a full vestured royal priesthood unto God.

Aaron and his sons, who represent the priesthood, were commanded to wear the following attire to minister unto the Lord:

The breast plate
The ephod
The robe of the ephod
The embroidered coat
The curious girdle
The breeches to cover their nakedness
The mitre
The crown with "Holy unto the Lord"

The breastplate worn over the embroidered coat consisted of jewels to represent each of the twelve tribes of Israel, which was worn over the chest of the priest. The ephod was essentially an apron worn over the coat. The hem of the ephod was trimmed with pomegranates and bells. The bells represent the gifts of the spirit and the pomegranates represent the fruit of the spirit, showing us it is the fruit of the spirit which cushion the gifts of the spirit, so that the giftings do not sound as a tinkling cymbal in the ear of God. The embroidered coat was for beauty and glory. I view the embroidery of the coat as the detailed, disciplined, intricate parts of your life that are finely woven into your character, reflecting the beauty of holiness, which brings glory unto

God. The curious girdle, which represents the private life of those who minister, being disciplined and tamed, was worn under the ephod. The breeches were worn to cover their nakedness. This is another example of the people covering the nakedness of the priesthood, even as Noah's two sons walked backward and covered his nakedness, unlike their brother, who told of his father's nakedness (faults) hilariously. The mitre (turban), representing the priesthood having a covering, was placed upon the head of the priest. The crown was placed over the mitre with the engraving HOLY UNTO THE LORD inscribed thereon, reflecting that our thought life and entire being is to be HOLY UNTO THE LORD.

~ *The Most Holy Place* ~

The priestly apparel was REQUIRED to enter into the Holy of Holies. Notice the combined skilled teamwork required in clothing the priesthood; ensuring the priest's entrance to and exit from the Most Holy Place. The combined skills were also required to build the tabernacle housing the presence of God. If all of these requirements were not met, the priest would have died upon entering the Most Holy Place.

Today we do not have a priest that is required to go into the Most Holy Place to make atonement for our sins. The sacrificial death of Jesus Christ has fulfilled the requirements for the remission of our sins. He is our high priest forever seated at the right hand of Father God. Now we can come boldly into His presence.

In addition **we are not a replacement for Israel**; however, the scriptures give us a pattern of how we may clothe the priest, and ultimately, the bride of Christ with our combined gifts and talents. It is in that unity that we will encounter more than the outer court experience of being forgiven and washed clean from dead trespasses and sins. Furthermore, we desire more than the inner court experience, a communion with Him at the table of shewbread, and the flickering of the revelation of God; a little here and a little there by the illumination of the candlestick. We want to present to Him a prepared priesthood, fully adorned, with full possession of the principle spices, having tried them by the fire, which burns all refuse and gives forth a sweet smelling savor. The bride of Christ, equipped with all of these elements to experience the grace to enter into the most holy place, will live in the manifestation of the glory of God in the earthly realm.

There are many gifts and skills within the body of Christ. Now is the hour that God is asking again of His people to bring your gifts and offerings to build His place of dwelling and prepare a royal priesthood, properly clothed to represent both God and man.

There are many possessing gifts now laid upon a shelf and do not perceive them as a potential asset to the body of Christ, but God is asking for us to dust them off and use them to build the tabernacle and clothe the priest. One may ask "How can my gift build Him a tabernacle or clothe the priest?" Your gifts and talents, combined with the fruit of the spirit, submitted as an offering along with the combined efforts of the other parts of the body of Christ, fitly joined together, provide a place of habitation for God. We thereby, cloth the priesthood with the proper attire to experience more than an outer court experience with God, or just an inner court experience with God. But through unity, we are armed to experience the third dimension that is beyond the veil. It is in the Most Holy Place that we experience that which cannot be produced by flesh. It was in the Most Holy Place that God met with man Spirit to spirit.

~ *Wise Hearted Menders* ~

Whether your gift is organizational skills, business, hospitality, domestic, sewing and crafts, child care and training, custodial, carpentry, counseling, cosmetology, horticultural, engineering, discipleship, writing, music, teaching, evangelism, prophecy, pastoral care, or apostolic (serve as a mitre, covering for other ministries), your offering is required to build the tabernacle and clothe the priest.

Imagine all of these different ministries presented unto God in their respective callings, building the tabernacle and clothing the priesthood. The effectiveness of this type of unity was seen when the wise hearted in the book of Exodus obeyed the word of the Lord from Moses and brought their gifts and talents to build the tabernacle and clothe the priest.

There are churches having all of the key elements required to enter into a more glorious realm of God, but lacking the finishing touches that the wise hearted add to the service. Have you ever attended a church service that had several of the key elements of success, but due to a lack of order, turned out to be less than a good memory? Have you ever visited a church which had wonderful music, great preaching, offered infant care, children's church, spiritual development classes, but was so disorderly that you could not enjoy the benefit that each of these much needed elements contributed to the service? The gift of the administrator is missing in this scenario. As we, the body of Christ, unify our gifts we are able to present a level of excellence that will bring honor unto the Lord.

Do you not know that when the appointed leader of your group represent, for example, the music department they are clothed in the gifting and skills of the combined work of every wise hearted member of the music department? The leader is clothed with every detail of the music secretarial staff, every written chart of music, every musician and instrument, the skills of the sound technician, the choir pastoral team who ministers to the needs of those in the music department, the sopranos, altos, and tenors that vocally accompany the lead worshipper, the individual displaying the lyrics of the song, and even the acceptance and unity of the congregation. All of these elements, supplied by the wise hearted, clothe the lead worshipper and equip them to escort the people of the Lord into a level of worship that can only be experienced beyond the veil.

On a larger scale, when your pastor ministers his breastplate is combined of every jewel, in the form of ministries and departments represented within your church. The combined efforts and excellence of each ministry clothe your pastor. Your combined effort either adorns them to enter into the third dimension of God or prohibits them from going beyond the veil of what flesh can produce. I am aware that a great responsibility is associated with the undergarments, representing the private life, of the priest. I am also aware that not having the combined efforts representing the other pieces of garments, jewels, representing the various groups of people in covenant with the ministry, and incense, the combined worship, may serve as an eliminating factor to entering into the third dimension.

When the various aspects of the ministry are woven together, it produces the priest's garments, serving as proper attire for the priest to minister in. When the minister proclaims the life giving word of God the anointing that has been ushered in by those worshiping with a wise heart, the administrative gifts (producing order), and those who have labored in intercession, permeating the atmosphere with the ointment of praise, anointing Him, provides direct access into the very presence of God.

I admonish you, if you have a pastor clothed with garments having holes of order, intercession, administrative gifts, hospitality gifts, biblical research gifts, take the time to inquire of the Lord how you may acquire His wise heart so that you may be used to mend and fill the gaps that expose the nakedness of the priesthood in your church.

Do not react like Noah's son Cush, and amusingly expose the nakedness seen with spiritual eyes. Be a wise hearted tailor and mend the priestly garment. A wise hearted individual would never say such things as *"His message lacked depth"*. The wise hearted would volunteer to be part of the biblical studies and research group, which submits history and current information for current and future series of teachings. This is one way to mend the priestly garment.

I will share with you one of my personal pet peeves. If your pastor is employed full time at a secular job, and also has the responsibilities of visiting the sick, the bereaved families, counseling, attending church business meetings, paying church bills, organizing Christian growth classes and mentoring leaders, they may not have the time required to research details and history for a sermon. It is easy to see how they may develop sicknesses designed to remove them from the earth prematurely. I can also see how they may have internal family problems stemming from a lack of time invested in their family.

I know some of you may be amazed to know that there are churches that actually have a non-salaried minister. If you are a part of a congregation having in the by laws of your assembly, a salary that is conducive to a comfortable lifestyle for the priesthood of your church, this thought may be foreign to you. I assure you providing a salary for the priesthood is a level of excellence and faith that many are yet aiming for.

God I pray that faith will arise in the heart of your people today to empower us to believe you to do what was originally purposed when you instructed Moses concerning the offering to sustain the priest and the tabernacle (church), so that ministers may live out their destiny and complete the work that you have assigned unto their hands.

~ *The Church at Large* ~

On a larger scale, as mentioned in the previous chapter, where we compared the body of Christ to David's sons, the various groups of the body of Christ can be viewed as part of the priestly garment. If we are to clothe Jesus, our high priest, properly in the earth today, we must present a combined work and skilled effort.

It is quite interesting God did not require all of the stones of the priest's breastplate to look alike or to be shaped the same, but He allowed each tribe to retain their unique nature, thereby keeping the individual properties of their stone. They were then placed inside a designed breastplate. Again the church does not replace the tribes of Israel; however, the pattern given to Moses serves as an example of how we, the church, are to present a combined work to clothe our High Priest. I see the various denominations and church groups as the stones finely woven together in the golden pure love of Christ, making up the breastplate of the Lord Jesus Christ.

The Father's appeal is being voiced again to prepare a spiritual breastplate, an ephod, and a robe, an embroidered coat, a miter, a girdle and breeches to clothe His royal priesthood properly in the earth, to allow access beyond the veil to a greater realm ever known before.

This type of unity produces the precious ointment upon the head (Christ) that and ran down upon the beard (matured ones) even Aaron's beard (the matured priesthood) to the skirts (the body of Christ) of his garments. It is the unity of each local church, then the unity of the combined portions of the body of Christ that ministers unto God. This anointing runs down to His priesthood, the matured wise hearted ones, down to his body, and there He commands the blessing.

 Selah

Chapter V

Joshua

~ *The Seventh Day* ~

Psalms 133:1 Behold, how good and how pleasant it is for brethren to dwell together in unity!
2 It is like the precious ointment upon the head, that ran down upon the beard, even Aaron's beard: that went down to the skirts of his garments;
3 As the dew of Hermon, and as the dew that descended upon the mountains of Zion: for there the LORD commanded the blessing, even life for evermore.

Joshua was given a great commission from God that you may identify with. Joshua was entrusted with the work and fruit of another servant's hand. It is always a challenge to step into the shoes of another with the commission to carry the work of the Lord to the next level.

To say the least, Joshua did not have an easy task. However, Joshua had the advantage of being a faithful minister to Moses during his leadership. It was Joshua (Exodus 17:9) that Moses assigned the duty of choosing men to go out with him to fight the Amalekites while he held the rod in his hand with Aaron and Hur by his side; thereby, God brought victory to Israel. Thereafter, God gave the first recorded words from Moses as a mentor to his successor; He would complete his battle.

This same servant of the Lord, Joshua, accompanied Moses as he went upon Mount Sinai for 46 days. For six days Moses and Joshua were enveloped in the glory of God. Joshua, as God's next leader, experienced the same glory as Moses while ministering to God's appointed leader and being tutored, mentored and nurtured to lead the next generation into the promises of God.

On the seventh day God called Moses out of the midst of the glory cloud to ascend the mountain and receive divine instructions for the receiving of gifts to make the tabernacle, priest's garment, ark of the covenant, table of shewbread, altar of burnt offerings, altar of incense, brass basin, and the oil of holy ointment. After 40 days, the first person to see Moses and the holy tablets God had written upon was Joshua.

One may ask: *What did Joshua do for 40 days as he waited for the appointed leader of the Lord to descend from the holy mountain of God?* He lived, moved, dwelt and breathed in THE GLORY OF GOD. Can you imagine 40 days in the visible, tangible GLORY OF GOD? I dare to say that not only did Moses have a divine appointment with God, but also likewise, Joshua had a divine appointment with God.

In Exodus 33:11, Joshua remained in the Tabernacle of the congregation, where the Lord would descend as a cloudy pillar and talk with Moses face to face. The scripture states that when Moses would go back to camp Joshua did not depart out of the Tabernacle of the congregation. The scripture does not say the glory ascended or departed as Moses left the Tabernacle of the congregation; therefore, I am inclined to believe that the cloudy pillar remained at the door while Joshua remained therein, abiding in the glory of God.

~ *Loyalty* ~

Joshua remained loyal to Moses through out his ministry. You won't ever find where Joshua spoke negative about his mentor Moses, or Zipporah, their children or the tribal elders. You will not find where Moses gave the instruction of the Lord, and Joshua privately or publicly mocked, or referred with sarcasm, to the instructions. You will not find where Moses presented the vision to possess the land, and Joshua disputed the vision of his leader. You will not find where Joshua entertained negative conversation with other elders, regarding Moses' leadership. You will not find where Joshua exposed Moses' character flaw (anger). You will not find where Joshua went to another leader, stating that he thought Moses could have utilized the sacrifices differently. In summation, you will not find where Joshua was disloyal. He not only was present and accounted for, but he was L-O-Y-A-L.

A person who craves the presence of God then pursues the presence of God, possessing loyalty for his mentor, is a prime candidate for promotion and blessings from God.

One of the blessings, which Joshua experienced, was leading a group of unified people. The same people who provoked Moses gave Joshua their loyalty and declared they would kill anyone who opposed Joshua (Joshua 1: 16-18).

The children of Israel made a decision to step into matured unity. Their maturity is seen when the manna ceased, and they did not cry for bread and water. This unity that Joshua experienced may have been the harvest from the seeds of loyalty he had sown into the life of Moses.

Transitions require a group effort. Transition is always an easier process when a future leader is mentored, equipped and the respect that they have for the leader is mirrored back into their life in the presence of the people. I love the fact that Moses gave Joshua authority over the armies and utilized his talents, *in his presence,* among the people. Nothing speaks louder of the authority given an individual, than the leader allowing that authority to be used in his presence. Notice Moses never publicly added to the decisions he gave Joshua the authority to make. Joshua was also publicly appointed as leader. This caused the people to respect him and adhere to his command.

~ *The Place of Commanded Blessing* ~

(Deuteronomy 34: 9) And Joshua the son of Nun was full of the spirit of wisdom; for Moses had laid his hands upon him: and the children of Israel hearkened unto him, and did as the LORD commanded Moses.

Joshua was given a fresh command, after the death of Moses, from God.

Josh 1:1 Now after the death of Moses the servant of the LORD it came to pass, that the LORD spake unto Joshua the son of Nun, Moses' minister, saying,
  2 Moses my servant is dead; now therefore arise, go over this Jordan, thou, and all this people, unto the land which I do give to them, even to the children of Israel.
  3 Every place that the sole of your foot shall tread upon, that have I given unto you, as I said unto Moses.
  5 There shall not any man be able to stand before thee all the days of thy life: as I was with Moses, so I will be with thee: I will not fail thee, nor forsake thee.
  6 Be strong and of a good courage: for unto this people shalt thou divide for an inheritance the

> *land, which I sware unto their fathers to give them.*
> *7 Only be thou strong and very courageous, that thou mayest observe to do according to all the law, which Moses my servant commanded thee: turn not from it to the right hand or to the left, that thou mayest prosper whithersoever thou goest.*

After these words Joshua and the Israelites stepped into the realm of unity which causes them to walk in the place of commanded blessing as described in Psalm 133:3.

> *3 As the dew of Hermon, and as the dew that descended upon the mountains of Zion: for there the LORD commanded the blessing, even life for evermore.*

Joshua's first command as the leader - *prepare for within three days we will go over Jordan.*

I dare to say unto you that the people of the Lord who will prepare and operate in unity, will experience what people have toiled, dreamed, hoped, and awaited for many years, and it shall be accomplished within days, while operating in the place of commanded blessing.

Joshua's second command - *Sanctify and cleanse yourself to see the wonders of God.*

If we are to see the manifested glory and wonders of God, we must, as the high priest, present ourselves Holy Unto The Lord. To begin this process, we must separate ourselves from any thing that is questionable in nature to the word of God. Pursue God. Spend time in the presence of the Lord daily through reading the Bible, singing songs unto the Lord, prayer and intercession, thanksgiving or worship. Adhere to the voice of the Lord by ridding your life of anything that He brings to your attention that is not pleasing to Him. Walk your life out daily as though it is your last day to love people and God. Separate, designate and live your life to be an extension of God, in the earth, to bring hope, faith, deliverance and God's love to people. This is a good place to start, and as you walk this out, He will show you a more excellent way to present yourself holy unto Him.

Thirdly Joshua prophesied - Declaring God would drive out their enemies and that Jordan, standing as an obstacle, would be cut off from the downward stream, allowing passage.

According to Dake's biblical notations, Jordan River is 150 to 200 miles long, 10 to 60 feet deep, and over flows its bank in March and April. It is presumed that the Israelites crossed during the flood season. Considering this information, it is easy to see how the Jordan could be viewed as an obstacle to the people of the Lord. Nevertheless, God had already given Joshua a word of victory regarding all opposing forces.

The children of Israel walked out the word of the Lord, crossing Jordan on dry ground. Forty thousand men, armed for war, led the people into the Jordan. The priest bearing the Ark of the Covenant preceded the people into the Jordan, clearing the way to the promises of God.

After all of the people crossed over, God commanded a representative from the twelve tribes of Israel to take stones from the midst of the Jordan, where the priest and the ark stood. Notice the scripture does not give an account of where God commanded Joshua to make a memorial to Him in the midst of the Jordan. One mark of a God appointed leader is they always go the extra sacrificial mile to please God. After the twelve tribal representatives had taken the commanded stones, Joshua then placed twelve stones in the midst of the Jordan. This is a prime example of the leader laying a fresh foundation of worship and a memorial unto God in the hard place.

The Lord seeks for a people who will, in unity, seek Him and with holy awe and reverence, build Him an altar on the throne of their hearts. God desires to place his abiding presence on the throne of our hearts not on a substation for Him to govern in our lives when we are in need of a miracle. God seeks for a people that He can bless and they not become worshippers of the blessings.

We find that the children of Israel remembered the Lord our God on their first night after crossing the Jordan. In fact, the twelve tribes placed their stones retrieved from the Jordan, at Gilgal, where they lodged that night. The stones of the tribes symbolized laying a fresh foundation on the threshold of inhabiting the promises of God. The stones also represented a memorial and testimony to the promises, faithfulness and covenant of God.

The children of Israel walked that day, in an anointing that is as the dew of Hermon and Zion. The dew upon Hermon and Zion is abundant even during dry weather. A referral to an anointing like the dew upon Hermon and Zion refers to an anointing that defies natural forces, which is what Israel experienced the day they crossed Jordan.

~ *Empowered Through Submission* ~

This same anointing gave them the grace to have prodigious faith and obedience towards God. Any true warrior, like Joshua, would know it is not naturally wise to render your army powerless before your enemies. Likewise, anyone that has followed God into unfamiliar territory would know that you can not lean solely on the arm of natural wisdom. It is during the times of your life, when you are in unfamiliar territory, that God will give you a command that goes totally against the wisdom of man. This is exactly what Joshua experienced when God told him, while in the territory of their enemies, to circumcise all of the males born in the wilderness. In effect, He told them, as a first fruit of entering into His manifested promise, to render themselves totally vulnerable and disabled as a natural symbol of the covenant, as He rolled away the 400 years of reproach in their spirit from slavery.

The children of Israel were empowered through submission unto the word of the Lord, through Joshua. In the book of Ephesians chapter 5, there is an exhortation from the writer, stating:

16 Redeeming the time, because the days are evil.

The first verses twenty-one through twenty-seven goes on to say:

21 Submitting yourselves one to another in the fear of God.
23 For the husband is the head of the wife, even as Christ is the head of the church: and he is the savior of the body.
24 Therefore as the church is subject unto Christ, so let the wives be to their own husbands in every thing.
25 Husbands, love your wives, even as Christ also loved the church, and gave himself for it;
26 That he might sanctify and cleanse it with the washing of water by the word,
27 That he might present it to himself a glorious church, not having spot, or wrinkle, or any such thing; but that it should be holy and without blemish.

These verses are rightfully used to instruct and give a foundation of order unto those in marriage. However, the same scripture can be used to instruct the body of Christ.

In verse 21 where we find, *"Submitting yourselves one to another,"* the instruction is first to the church.

If we are to ever come to full maturity and gather a full harvest we must discipline ourselves to come under the covering of submission. It is through submission that we uncover dormant resistance to authority. Every army that functions properly, executing the assigned task with as few casualties as possible, is an army that operates in submission to authority. We must be a body of believers, unified; not to build our own kingdom, as was the case of the tower of Babel. The people at the Tower of Babel were void of the approval of God, attempting to accomplish their own vision rather than accomplishing His vision. Our main goal must be the completion of His assignment for the portion of the body of Christ that He has assigned us to serve. This is the type of submission the Children of Israel had towards Joshua and the command of the Lord spoken through him.

After crossing the Jordan, the mindset of the people was to complete the will of God, concerning possessing the land of promise. With this type of unity, they were positioned to see the miraculous hand of God and His glory revealed.

~ *The Captain of the Host* ~

It is not unusual, at new thresholds of manifested promises, to receive what is perceived as an untimely command from God, that renders you utterly helpless - requiring you to trust Him, seek Him, lean on Him, depending on Him and His grace, more than ever before.

It is at that moment of vulnerability that the Captain of the host (Jehovah-Sabaoth) appeared unto Joshua. It is in the hour you are disarmed, in accordance with your obedience unto God, prostrate in worship, He will show up to give you instructions that will thrust you into your destined victory.

The Lord spoke unto Joshua, in his state of vulnerability, for all of his men of valor were recovering from circumcision, saying:

> *Joshua 6: 2 And the LORD said unto Joshua, See, I have given into thine hand Jericho, and the king thereof, and the mighty men of valor.*
> *3 And ye shall compass the city, all ye men of war, and go round about the city once. Thus shalt thou do six days.*
> *4 And seven priests shall bear before the ark seven trumpets of rams' horns: and the seventh day ye shall compass the city seven times, and the priests shall blow with the trumpets.*
> *5 And it shall come to pass, that when they make a long blast with the ram's horn, and when ye hear the sound of the trumpet, all the people shall shout with a great shout; and the wall of the city shall fall down flat, and the people shall ascend up every man straight before him.*
> *6 And Joshua the son of Nun called the priests, and said unto them, Take up the ark of the covenant, and let seven priests bear seven trumpets of rams' horns before the ark of the LORD.*
> *7 And he said unto the people, Pass on, and compass the city, and let him that is armed pass on before the ark of the LORD.*

Things to notice in the second verse while Joshua was in God's presence; He told him that He had already given him Jericho, the king, and the men of valor. This was before any men of war had assembled, before any trumpets were blown, and before Jericho's walls fell.

Things to notice in verse three, first compass the city - mark your territory. Second, men of war - represents the people of the Lord. Third, six days - six, the number of man. Six days, the number of creation.

Things to notice in verse four; first the number seven is the number of perfection. Second, The Ark of the Covenant is symbolic of God among his people. Third, the Ram is an animal of sacrifice. Fourth, the horn is a symbol of anointing or instrument of anointing, praise, and judgment. Fifth, the seventh day is a day of rest, day of completion and perfection. Sixth, the priest is God's appointed and anointed servant.

The order of their procession was, first, the priest passed before the Ark of the Covenant, blowing the trumpets. It seems as if, while the priest blew the trumpets, the armed men went out before them, then the priest followed the armed men, thereafter, were those carrying the ark of the covenant, and following the ark were the remaining men of valor, which took up the rear.

I find very interesting the instructions of the Lord. God told them to march around the walls one time for six days and on the seventh day march around the wall seven times. He further instructs them to bear before the ark seven priests, with seven trumpets of rams' horns.

As the priest began to blow the horn; the men of valor walked through the strength of the sound of anointed praise, proceeding to the front of the procession.

Envision the sound of praise coming from the ram's (a sacrifice) horn (praise) as a mist. Now, see the men of valor's armor, saturated with the dew of sacrificed praise, as they walk through the mist.

In this unity, we have seven priests each blowing a ram's horn. (As stated the number seven represents rest, perfection and completion.) This symbolizes a perfected priesthood, armed with a perfected praise. This united effort prepared incense of praise for the presence of God, which was the Ark of the Covenant, to walk through.

For six days this procession marched around the walls of Jericho. Being that six is the number of man, the six days symbolize the effort and obedience of man. It is when we are given an assignment from God, and it is carried out in obedience, that we position ourselves to see the power of God manifested on a level that is beyond the natural realm of what man can produce. Indeed it is not natural; it is supernatural.

The seventh day, God commanded the procession would circle the walls seven times. I see this seventh day as a day of supernatural unity, protection, strength, rest and victory.

It was on the seventh day that the armies of Israel had more opportunities to be overtaken by discord. Any time groups of people are carrying out an assignment by God that is foreign (not given before) to them, there is always an occasion for the followers to question the practicality of such actions. If the seventh day of their march was on the Sabbath, one could have reasonably posed a question such as, "If the order was given by God, why would He tell us to carry out this laborious practice on a day of rest?" The children of Israel were on unfamiliar soil, carrying out an act that went against their "religious" practice. It is on the seventh day, or days of completion, that we must hear the progressive word of the Lord that often goes against religious practices. An example of supernatural unity is seen on the seventh day.

It was also the seventh day the armies of Jericho had more opportunities to attack, while the Israelites encompassed the walls. On the seventh day, the armies of Israel were in a vulnerable position for a longer period of time. For an army to allow themselves to be exposed before their enemies the length of time necessary to walk around a city seven times requires the supernatural protection of God.

The physical strength of the children of Israel was challenged on the seventh day. It is said, by some theologians, that the exact size of the city is not known. As an example, if the circumference of the city were three miles, then seven times around the city would be twenty-one miles. Twenty-one miles of travel by foot is a long enough span of time to become weary. The seven times around the city was to be completed in one day while the seven priest are carrying the ram's horn, the bearers of the ark are carrying the weight of the presence of God in shittim wood overlaid with gold, and the men of valor are carrying out the seemingly menial task of walking. These are the hours that you surpass your natural strength and rely totally upon the supernatural strength of God.

It was in those last hours of obedience; the children of Israel were literally walking into their predestined victory. Finally on the seventh day, after the seven times around the city was completed, the children of Israel, walking in the supernatural strength of God, carried out the last command to blow the trumpets and lift their voice in a shout that through the power of God brought the walls of Jericho down. Thereafter, Israel's men of valor overtook the men of Jericho, realizing their long awaited victory, as the dust settled in the place of commanded blessing.

~ *Our Seventh Day* ~

According to most theologians, there are four thousand years from Adam to Jesus. It has been over two thousand years since Jesus gave His life on Calvary's cross. Ever since the ascension of Christ, the question has been raised concerning his return. The apostle Peter addresses those who have questioned the elapsed time for the coming of the Lord.

II Peter 3:8 But, beloved, be not ignorant of this one thing, that one day is with the Lord as a thousand years, and a thousand years as one day.

It is within this revealed truth of God we locate the day we are currently living in. We know that 4,000 + 2,000 = 6,000. If one day is as a thousand years and a thousand years is as one day and 6,000 years (6 days God's time) has passed, we are living in the beginning of the seventh day.

Please understand the prophetic depth of the seventh day we are now living in. This is the day that God will command the body of Christ to walk in unity on a level not known before, and we will defy natural forces that stand as obstacles. In obedience to the command of God the body of Christ is entering into a level of unity, where we have, across the globe, in submission to God, rendered ourselves vulnerable for His purpose. He is unveiling his plan, giving us directions that will thrust us into a victory, in which we will accomplish seven times more in one day, than was accomplished in any one of the previous six days (6,000 years). Furthermore, we will accomplish more in this one day than was accomplished in the combined six days.

This is the day of the unified body, where every portion will walk in their divine expertise. Like the men of valor, we will yield forth the perfected praise, birthed out of a perfected sacrifice, as seen with the seven ram's horns, led by the perfected priesthood. We will see where the body has clothed the priest, God, on the earth with their gifts and talents. We will see the presence of God in an elevated position, as seen with the carriers of the ark, above ALL else. The body of Christ will experience supernatural strength, as we are aligned with His will, to carry out *all* that He has commanded. And finally, this is the day we will experience the **GLORY** of God with signs, wonders, creative miracles and victories that can not be linked to the hand of man, for the Captain of the Host shall do His work in the earth, producing our predestined victory in The Place of Commanded Blessing, Unity.

~~~~~~~~~~~~~~~~~~ Selah ~~~~~~~~~~~~~~~~~~

~ *Final Words* ~

It is my desire that this book has compelled your heart to earnestly contend for The Place of Commanded Blessing, Unity. Unity occurs on purpose and purpose occurs upon the fertile soil of Unity. The purpose of Unity in the body of Christ is to accomplish God's given task. I am grateful for the opportunity to have shared with you examples of Unity, through the pavements of suffering, in the lives of the Early Church and also seen in lives of David, Moses and Joshua. God is seeking for people who will unite their forces to glorify Him in the earth. I pray from this day forward you will walk in The Place of Commanded Blessing, Unity.

Sharon Rich

~ *Sources* ~

Forbush, William, ed. *Fox's Book of Martyrs*. Crosswalk.com. Copyright 1995-2007. http://www.crosswalk.com

Hinn, Benny. *The Tabernacle.* Videocassette. BennyHinn Ministries, 1994.

Hinn, William. *How the Anointing Flows in Your Life.* Audiocassette. Resurrection Life Ministries, 2001.

Merriam Webster's Collegiate Dictionary. Tenth Ed. Springfield, MA: Merriam Webster, Incorporated, 1994.

Religious Tolerance. *Ontario Consultants on Religious Tolerance.* May 1995. http://www.religioustolerance.org

Strong, James. *Strong's Exhaustive Concordance of the Bible.* World Bible Publishers, 1980, 1986. CDROM. Quickverse 4.0 Parsons Technology, 1996.

Vine, William Edwy; Unger, Merrill Federick; and White, William. *Vine's Complete Expository Dictionary of Old and New Testament Words*. One-Volume Edition. New York: Thomas Nelson Publisher, 1985.